AF422858

Section Two: *Family*

Section Three: *Life*

<h1 style="text-align:center">Section Four: Life 2020</h1>

Preface

I composed my first poem at the age of four. It simply said,

> _Beware of the little white dove._
> _Because he's coming for all of your love._

It was just two lines that I put into a melody and would sing over and over and again.

Years later, when I was a freshman in High School, I wrote this report on poetry. And now, again years later, I believe it still holds true today.

My 1976 World:
What's Important to Me
and My Generation in Poetry.

What is poetry? This is answered easily enough. The reader can tell by the page's appearance whether he or she is reading poetry or not. Poetry can also be very deceiving. Some so-called poetry is not really poetry at all, and then there is some that looks and sounds like prose.

Poets of all ages often use the moods they sense to inspire poetry of different subjects. Sometimes poets write of things they see or experience. Frequently poets will let their imaginations run wild and this causes them to see *things entirely different from other people. This usually results in an imaginary or eccentric poem.*

Most people and especially people around my age often use poetry to express their feelings. If they write poetry, they might write something to describe the way they feel inside. They either come out and say what they feel or use symbols to represent their emotions. If people my age want to tell someone something they feel or believe in, they might find a suitable poem and give it to this person.

Poetry also makes erudition more interesting and memorable. Take Henry Wadsworth Longfellow's poem "Paul Revere's Ride" for example. Poetry puts the events in a special order and makes them more exciting and less boring to read. So therefore, the students learn more from reading the poems than they do from reading about events in History books.

Of course, there are students who are not fond of poetry at all, but the ones who have discovered its distinguished qualities find it pretty, most relaxing, and rewarding.

To Love a Poet

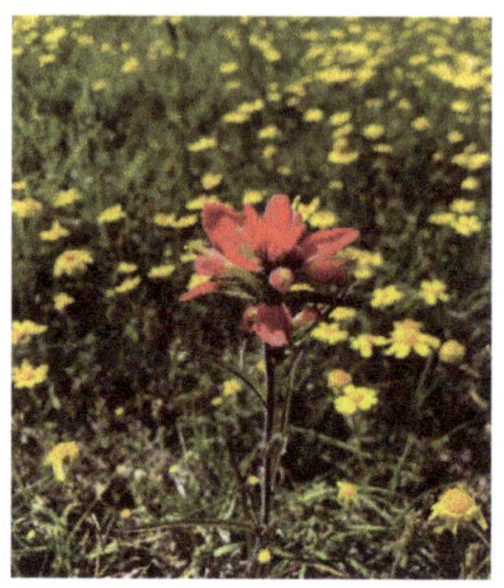

To love a poet is to love out loud.
In a way full of mystery and hue.
Because to love a poet,
Is to love someone unique,
Full of colors like red, green, and blue.
To write as a poet is to write in dimensions,
Of the world, land, sea, and sky.
And to write as a poet,
Is to write full of emotion,
And to tell your reader why.
To live as a poet is to live full of feelings,
Feelings of every design.
To be a poet gives way to writing,
In a style that's truly mine.
I love to write as a poet does,
And to gather every line through life.
To express myself in magical ways,
Ways that come from truth, joy, and strife.

God

The grace of the Lord Jesus Christ and the love of God and the fellowship of the Holy Spirit be with you all (2 Corinthians 13:14 ESV).

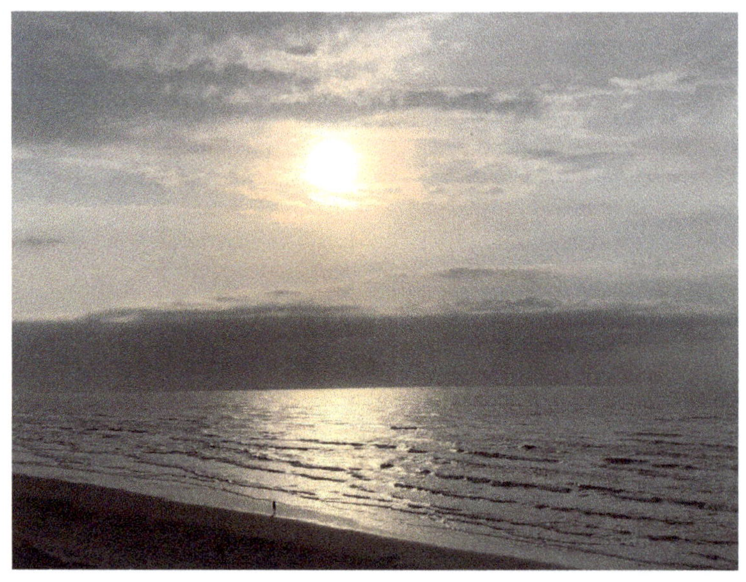

This Little Light

Do you remember the song,
"This Little Light of Mine,
I'm going to let it Shine?"
Do you remember the day you met Jesus?
Let me tell you about mine.

While sitting in a bathtub,
Distraught and weeping under the water.
I prayed to God,
To know His son, Jesus!
It was a moment like no other.

The water was not holy.
It was not even clean.
But when I came up,
After meeting Jesus,
I felt the purist love I had ever seen.

I know that day in that tub,
My life was changed forever.
I knew that things,
Would never be the same.
They would be so much better.

This little light of mine,
I'm going to let it shine.
Thank you, God,
For now, and forever
For making Jesus mine.

This little light of mine,
I'm going to let it shine.
Do you remember the day?
You can say,
I made Jesus mine.

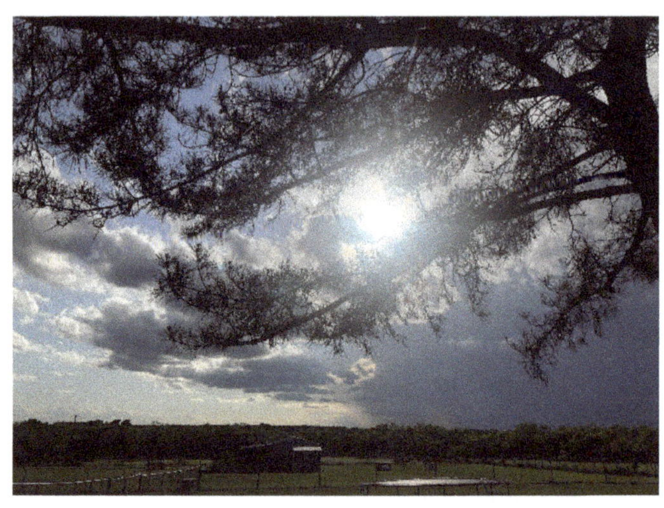

In My Heart

As a little one,
I screamed inside.
The pain was so deep.
And I could not hide.

It built over days,
Weeks, months, and years.
There was nothing to do.
To dry the tears.

I now scream inside,
For every other little one.
That will feel that pain.
With nowhere to run.

Lord, help them know.
They have a place with You.
And one day they'll go to it.
All happy and new.

In my heart,
The sadness continues to build.
I continue to wait.
For the pain to yield.

In my heart,
I'm screaming inside.
Waiting, just waiting,
For the pain to subside.

I know not to look,
Anywhere but above.
That's the only place.
To find healing love.

Heavenly Father, please,
In me dwell.
Strengthen my heart!
And make it well.

I'm screaming inside.
Lord, draw me near.
Guide my path.
Make your Word clear.

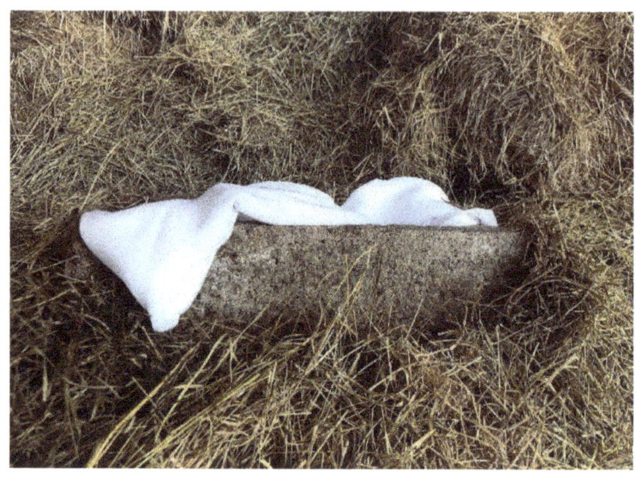

They Named Him Jesus

A baby boy was born that day,
Not to want and not to play.
A big job He came to do,
To save the world, me, and you.
He grew up strong to share His Father's love.
He came to love us from above.
The name He was given was Jesus, King.
A light for salvation He did bring.
He's my savior, and he wants to be yours too.
For He came and gave all for me and you.

There is no picture that can truly describe what Jesus
did for us, but we can see what little we did for Him.

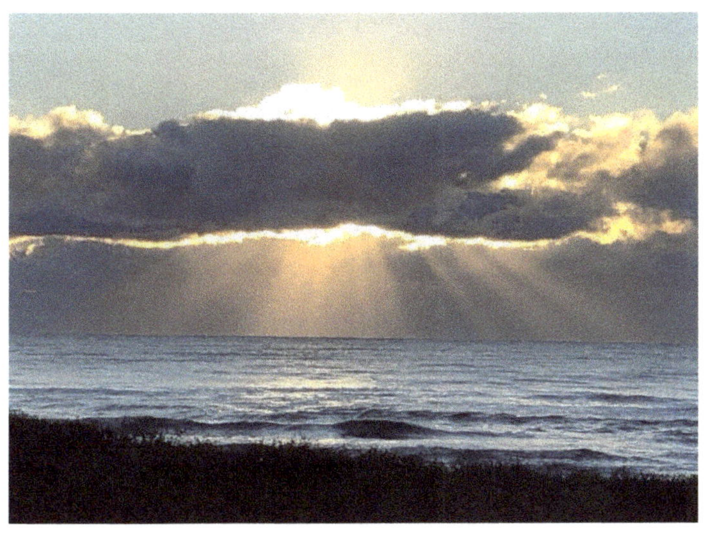

Blessings

*Thus says the Lord: "Stand by the roads, and look,
and ask for the ancient paths, where the good way
is; and walk in it, and find rest for your souls"
(Jeremiah 6:16 ESV).*

Oh, the blessings we receive!
When we turn to God and believe.
Even through those times of sorrow,
He promises us a heavenly tomorrow.

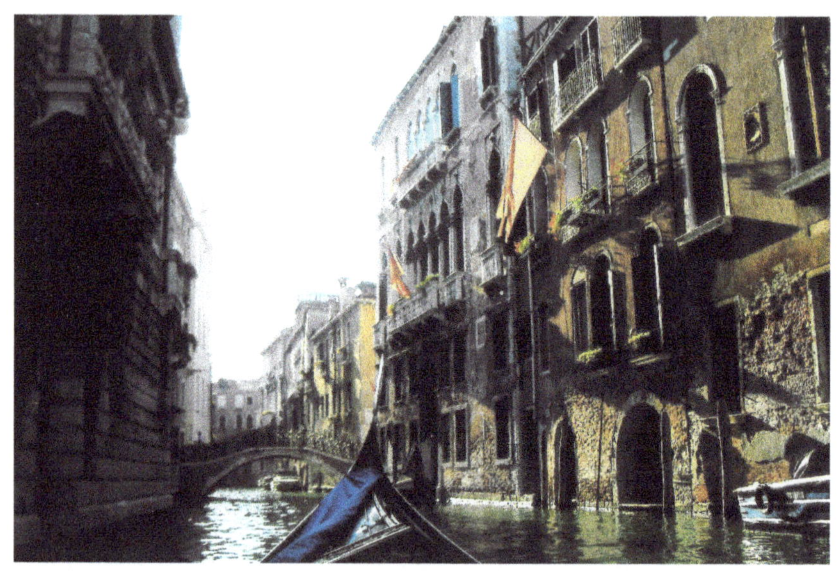

A Silent Dream

A silent dream I never told.
But my loving Savior,
Did the secret hold.
In a way that seemed impossible,
A way I would have never thought.
He gave me the moment and the reason.
And the guidance for the tickets to be bought.
So off to Italy, one son in hand,
To see the other,
Play at Perugia in the Jazz Band.
The blessings bestowed on those days long stay.
Only my loving Savior
Could have paved the way.
God wants us happy.
He wants to give us joy.
He gave us His ultimate gift.
In His own baby boy.

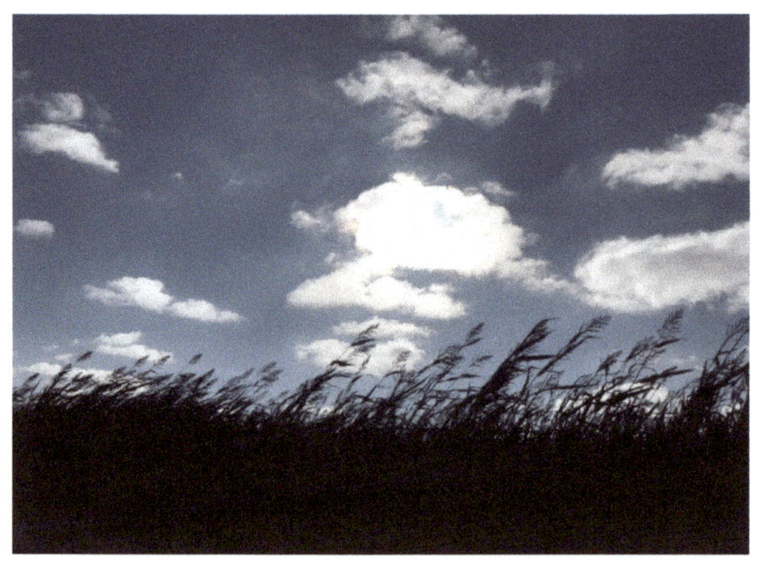

Subtle Sounds

"The wind blows where it wishes, and you hear its sound, but you do not know where it comes from or where it goes. So it is with everyone who is born of the Spirit" (John 3:8 ESV).

Do you hear the subtle sounds I hear?

I hear subtle sounds not everyone hears.
The electricity surge as I turn on the switch.
My knife blade slicing on the cutting board.
I hear the spiderweb break as I tear it apart.

What are the subtle sounds you hear each day?

I hear the subtle hum of the refrigerator.
The hum of the CD player as it sits idle but on.
The subtle sound of my husband's footsteps.
The water trickling through the water hose.

When do you hear subtle sounds the most?

I hear crickets chirping, wind swishing.
The subtle sounds of morning.
The subtle sounds of evening.
The quiet subtle sound of night.

Where are you when you hear subtle sounds?

I hear them in the waves of the ocean.
I hear them when the wheat and corn blow.
I hear subtle sounds as I sit in my house.
I hear them when my prayers are for you.

Do you hear the subtle sound of our Savior calling?

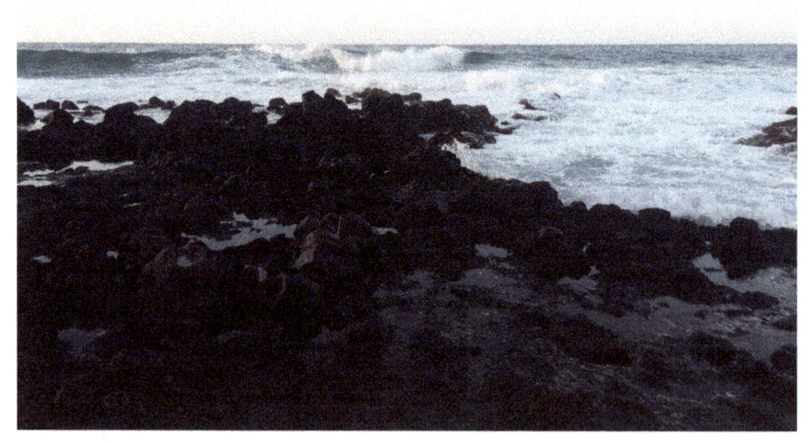

Waves Rushing In

The waves rushing in never stop.
So does my love for you.

The waves rushing in change the shore.
Making it all anew.

You have changed my life and washed me clean.
Giving me a new way to go.

You led me from the life I was drowning in,
And the sin that anchored me so.

My love is rushing like the ocean's waves.
I cannot contain my heart.

My heart is heightened like the cresting waves.
From You I will not depart.

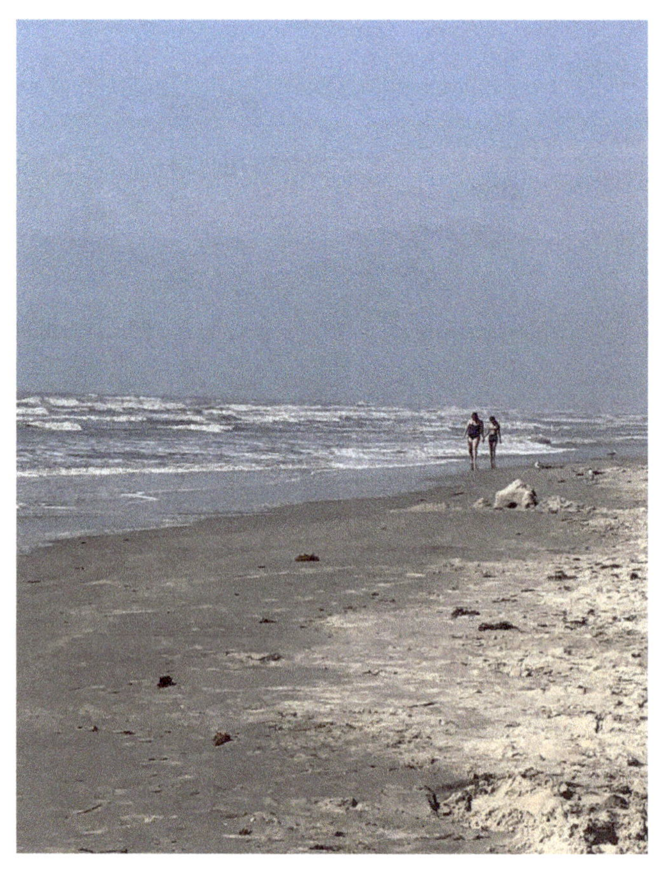

From the Depth of My Heart

I never knew how much they meant to me,
Until they were not there.
I prayed, I pleaded, I needed to know.
Where my life would go.
I asked, "Where, oh where."

God was good, He never let go.
He only allowed the hurt so deep.
Not too deep I could not hold on.
So, I learned to give my hurt to Him.
And then bow my head and weep.

The past is over, it is long ago,
Now forever behind in my thoughts.
But I will never forget.
And I will always be ready,
To put God first where I ought.

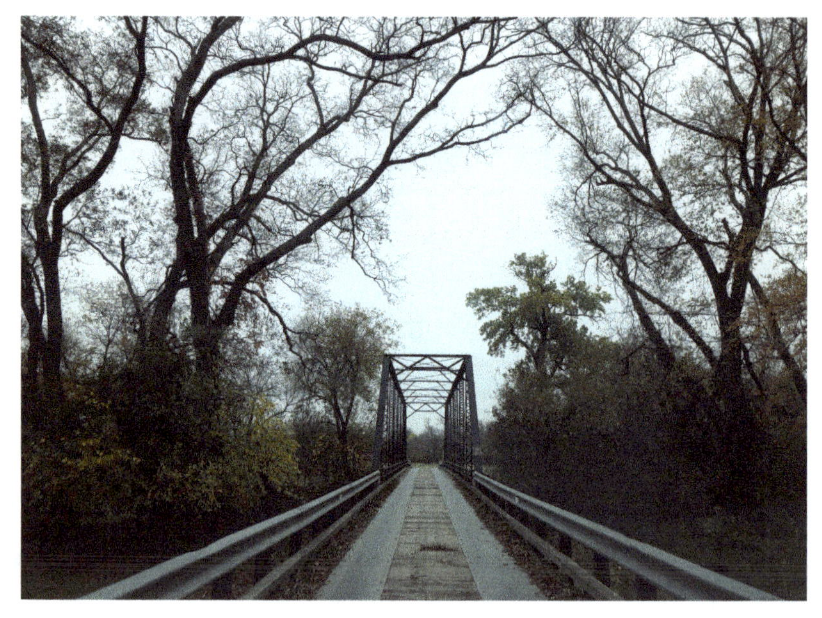

Your Love, Your Wrath

Come to me, Lord, and heal my hurts.
Take me in your arms and guide my path.
I'll wait for you and the justice you'll give.
I'll wait for you to deliver wrath.

My life longs for peace, love, and joy.
I'm free when I listen and follow you.
I know to pray for and love my enemies.
For you have blessed my heart and made it new.

I used to be just like the worst,
My heart was full of sin.
But Jesus came and washed it all away,
And my new life was able to begin.

So, I'll wait for you and your justice.
I'll let you be the one to deliver wrath.
I'll live with your promises and your joy.
And let your word, Lord, guide my path.

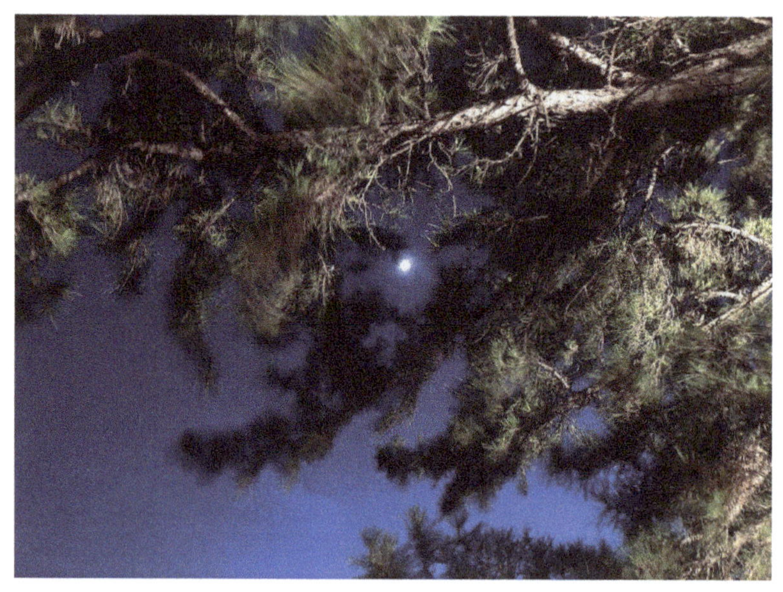

Sun and Stars

The sun and the moon look to the stars.
And the stars look back at them.
They all know from whom they came.
And that they lead us back to Him.

The flowers open and their beauty we see.
We need to wonder no more.
Our God has given us His imprint everywhere.
He is with us now like before.

Wake me up Lord, wake me now.
Show me where to go and what to do!
I need to hear your instructions.
And tell me how to know it's from you.

Wake me up Lord to see your beauty.
I want to see and hear.
I want to see your stars and flowers.
And to feel your presence always near.

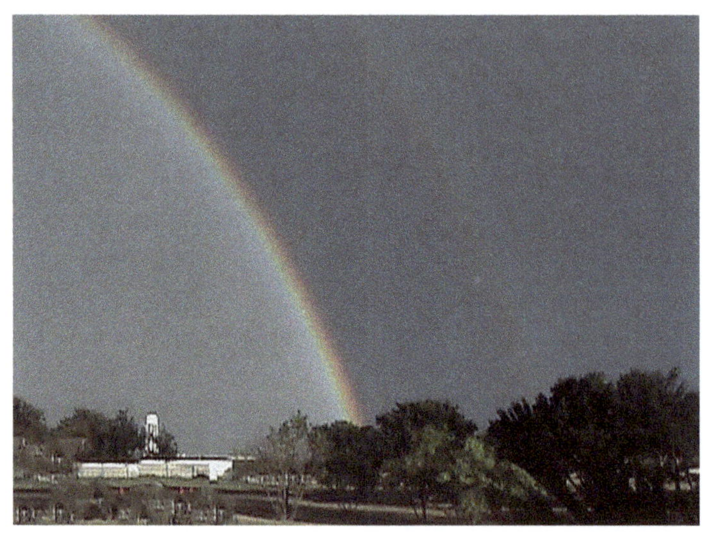

Our Gift Fully from God

*For those who live according to the
flesh set their minds on the things of the
flesh, but those who live according to
the Spirit set their minds on the things
of the Spirit (Romans 8:5 ESV).*

Jesus came, bled, and died.
For us to know His Father fully.
What are we willing to fully give?
To be with Him eternally.

And once we know Jesus,
God gives His spirit as our guide.
Who loves us and leads us perfectly.
It is in Him I will fully abide.

God, Jesus, and the Holy Spirit,
Are the three I will fully submit to.
I gave my all, and asked for forgiveness,
And He made me fully new.

After we know Jesus and are given His Holy Spirit as a gift, His Spirit is with us the most, and it's this Spirit that seems to be mentioned the least. He's a gift to always remember.

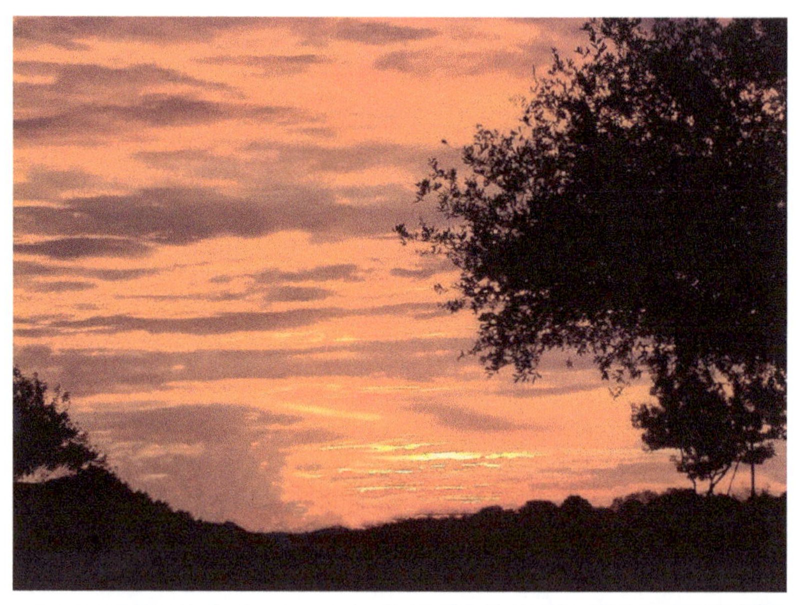

Jesus

The whips I endured on my back,
Did not even compare,
To the ones,
My Savior went through.

And the pain l felt,
Was absolutely nothing.
Compared to the pain,
Jesus knew.

There's so much sadness in our world,
Homelessness and discontent.
I know the things Jesus said to us.
And I know more now about what He meant.

My heart goes out, it aches, it cries.
For the ones I see in pain.
I wish that somehow, I could help them see.
It will all one day be for gain.

My prayer is that you could see it too,
And feel it in your heart.
We need to mend, to heal, and smile.
And give life with God a start.

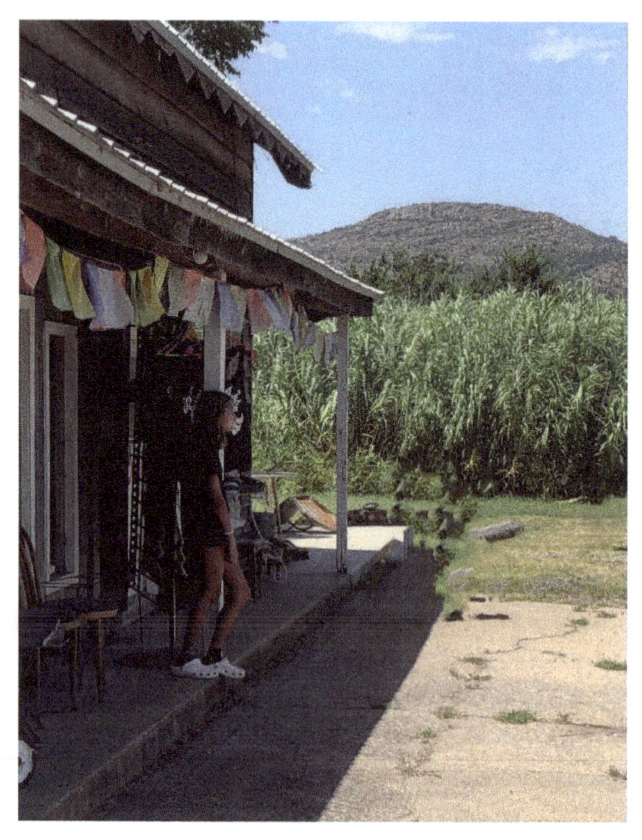

Shady Lady

Shady lady, come on by.
Let me tell you a story or two.
Shady lady, look up high.
I'll tell you what the Lord can do.

Run towards God,
And forget your ways.
He will forgive you,
And will bless your days.

So, shady lady, come on by.
I'll give you the Gospel now.
It tells you about knowing Jesus.
And it also tells you how.

Shady lady, what do you say,
Would you like to come and chat?
God gives the gift of love and guidance,
Through His Holy Spirit, and He's good at that.

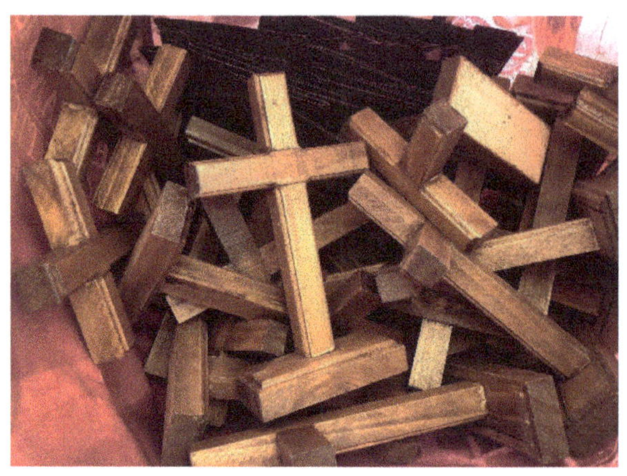

My Soul Wrenches

My soul wrenches.
For the future.
The future for my kids and grandkids.

My soul wrenches.
For the past.
For those that mourned and lived in sorrow.

My soul wrenches.
For the present.
For you now to know Jesus.

He is the only light.
And the only way to eternity.
For Him my soul wrenches.

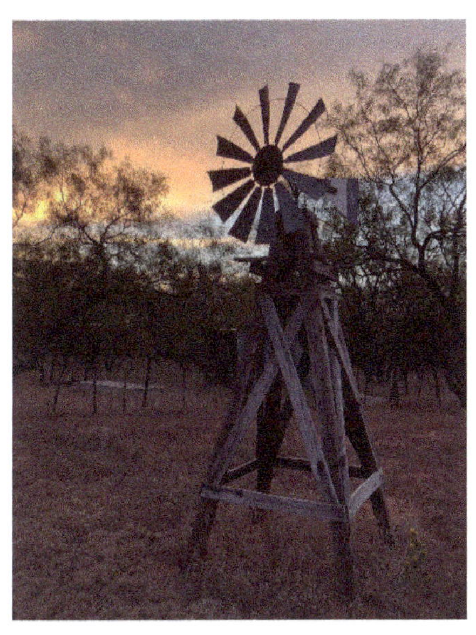

Like
the
Windmill

Like the windmill,
Goes around and around,
Forever in its place.
I see time slipping by fast.
It's like we're all in a race.
The windmill's shadow,
Is soft and fleeting,
It moves by with the sun.
Our time for God's grace,
Moves as such,
There once and for all,
Then done.

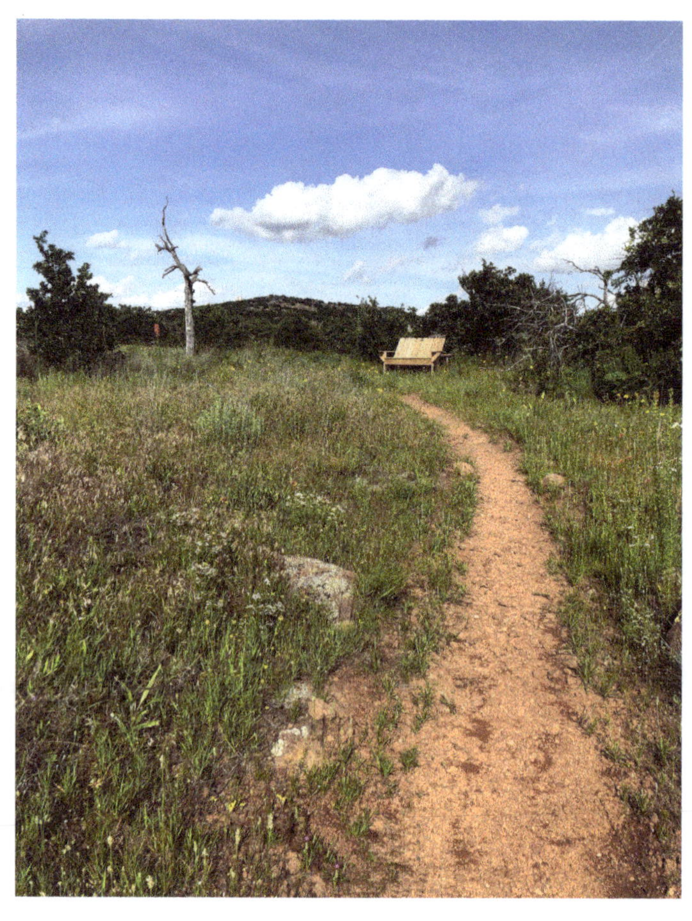

The Resting Place

There is a resting place,
At the end of the path
It's where I can sit
And be out of the world's wrath.

My God is with me
Listening to my woes
And everything in my heart
He already knows.

Yes, the place on the path
Has a cozy welcoming bench
Where I can sit
And let my soul vent.

I'll go there often
As often as I can
I'll sit with my Lord
And rest in His hands.

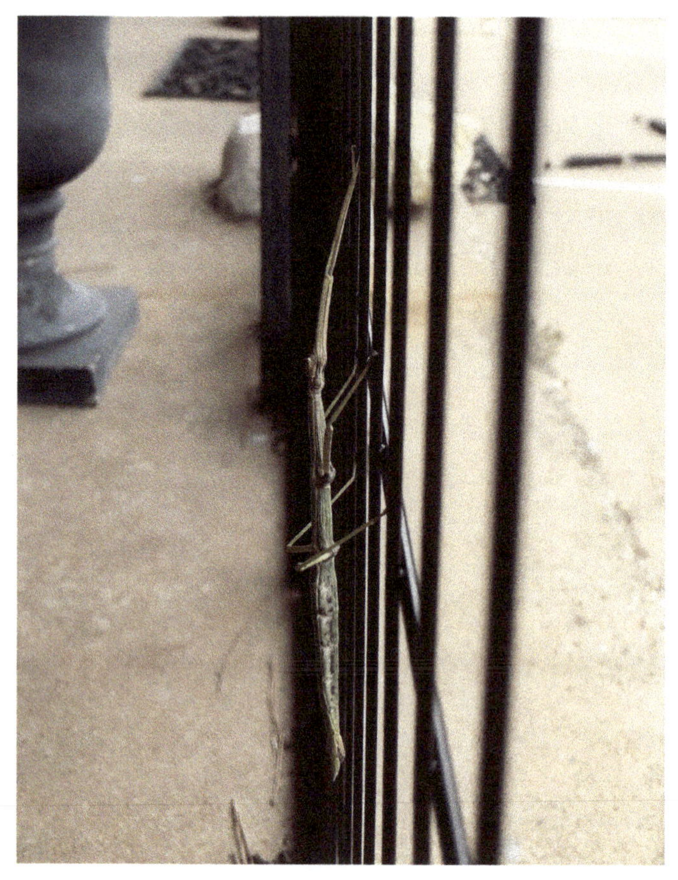

Oddities

I have always found beauty in the oddest places,
I'm glad our God does too.
I know this is true and that He does this.
For He found beauty in me and you.

I look at something old and broken,
And know it was meant to be.
It started out as a beautiful creation,
And it still is if we open our eyes and see.

So, whatever it is,
It shows His glory from above.
And whether it's an item, object, alive or not,
Realize He made them all from love.

Jesus in the Clouds

They said they saw Jesus in the clouds.
And I did not debate.
The world may not believe,
But He was there for their sake.

I told them when I saw Jesus,
Walking by the window.
He did it on a day He felt,
His presence I needed to know.

All our faith was strengthened,
That day we shared our beliefs.
And Jesus led the way,
Leading our faith to increase.

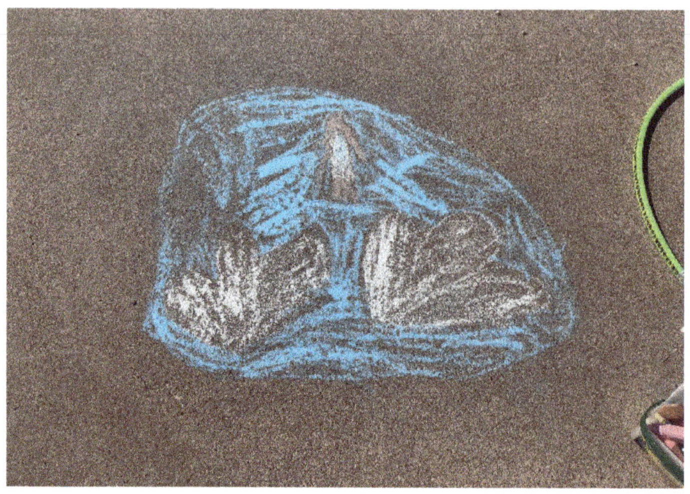

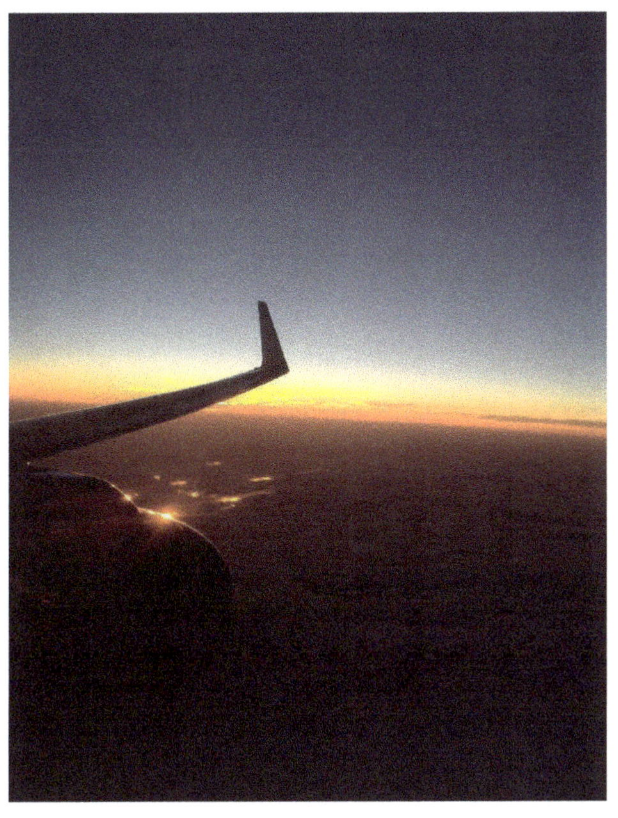

A Prayer

Wherever I am,
I feel your splendor.
I see and know you are there.
Your bigness and grace surround me.
I thank you, Lord, and I love you.
You truly are our magnificent God!

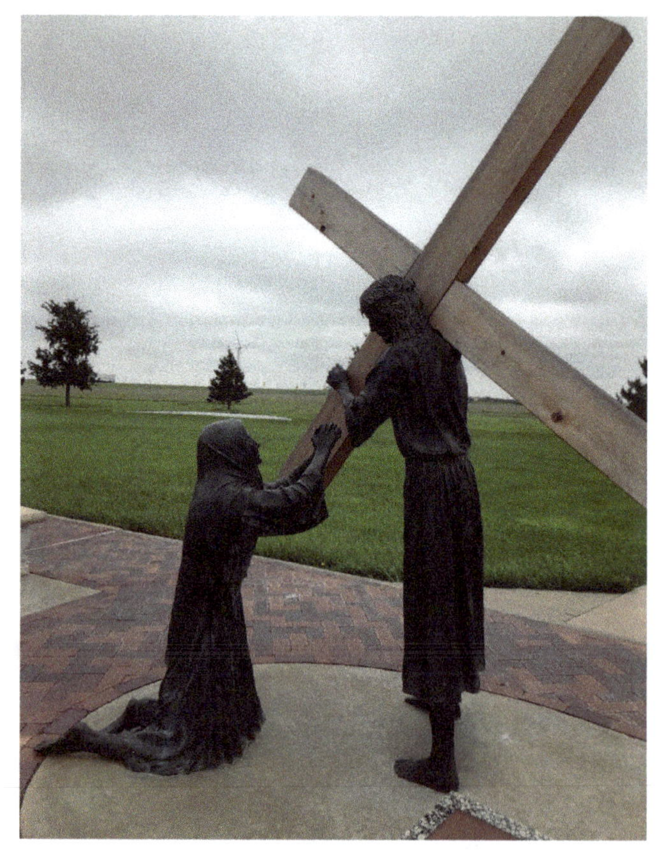

A Broken People

We are a broken people.
And the one holding the glue is God.

Mend us, Lord?

Put our broken pieces back together.
Be the bond that completes us,
And makes us whole.
Without you, Heavenly Father,
I am nothing and continue to break.
Only with your son,
Can I be bonded with you!

Mend us, Lord, mend us, Jesus.
Give us your Spirit to bond us together.

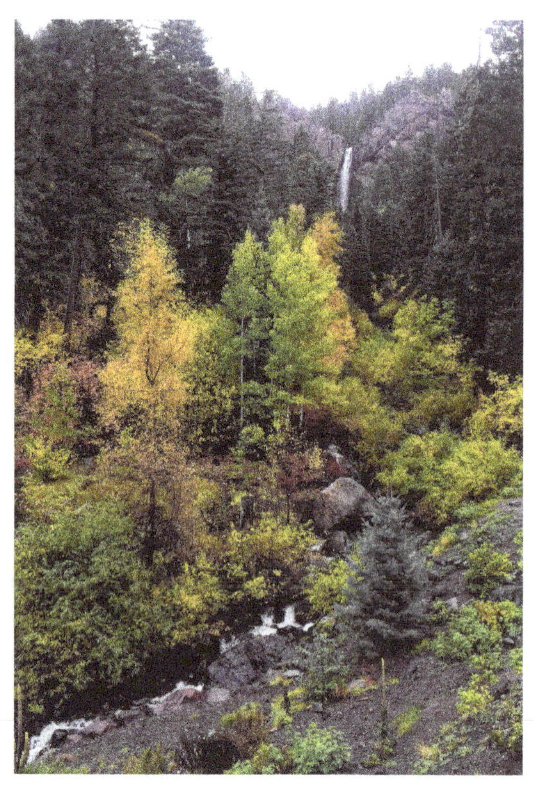

Smells of Wonder

I walk in wonder of the smells from the trees so tall.
I wish I could send them to you as I walk in awe.
The birds are chirping, the wind is calm.
God is there as we're told in the 139th of Psalm.
I follow the smells down the hill and then I hear its
sound.
A small but lovely flowing creek just waiting to be
found.
And from the top of the hill, the prettiest sight,
With flowers, big trees and rocks, until I looked
further below.
And the refuse I saw angered my heart and brought
sorrow for me to know.
I noticed close by the piling of brush and gravel
making a path to clear.
I knew the work was to restore, and the beauty was
once again near.
I let the wonder smells guide me home knowing
beauty would come again.
I prayed, I thought, how blessed I was, to see this
beauty from within.

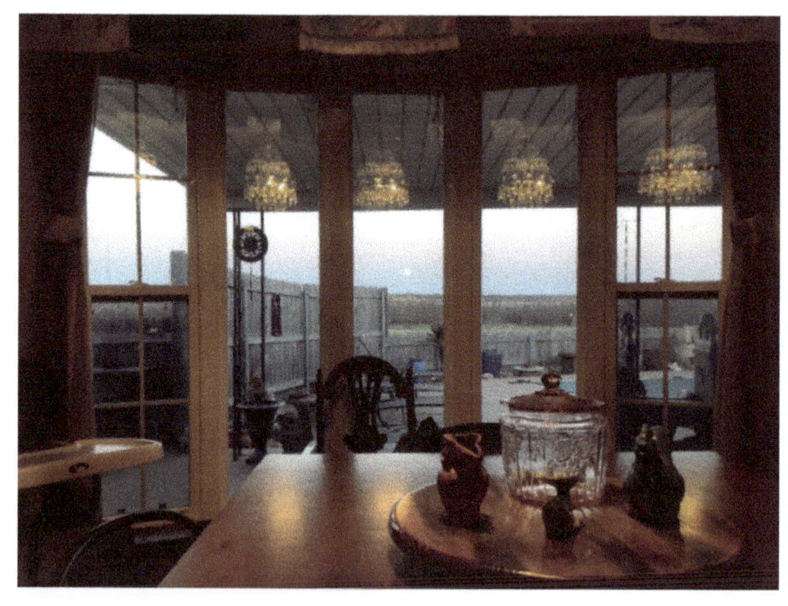

The View

How can I be sad?
When I look at the view of God's world.
I see the beauty within.

I see the trees,
That He made so perfectly,
With every limb's twist and turn.

I see the colors of their leaves,
As the seasons change.
They remind me of each holiday to come.

I see the lake with its water swelling in the wind,
Sometimes with white caps.
It helps me know how hard the wind blows.

I have seen the times the lake dried up,
And I know God was saying it would be ok.
He had everything under control.

I see God's world in the view out my window,
Past my table and chairs.
I see beyond my back patio and yard,
And I know God is always there.

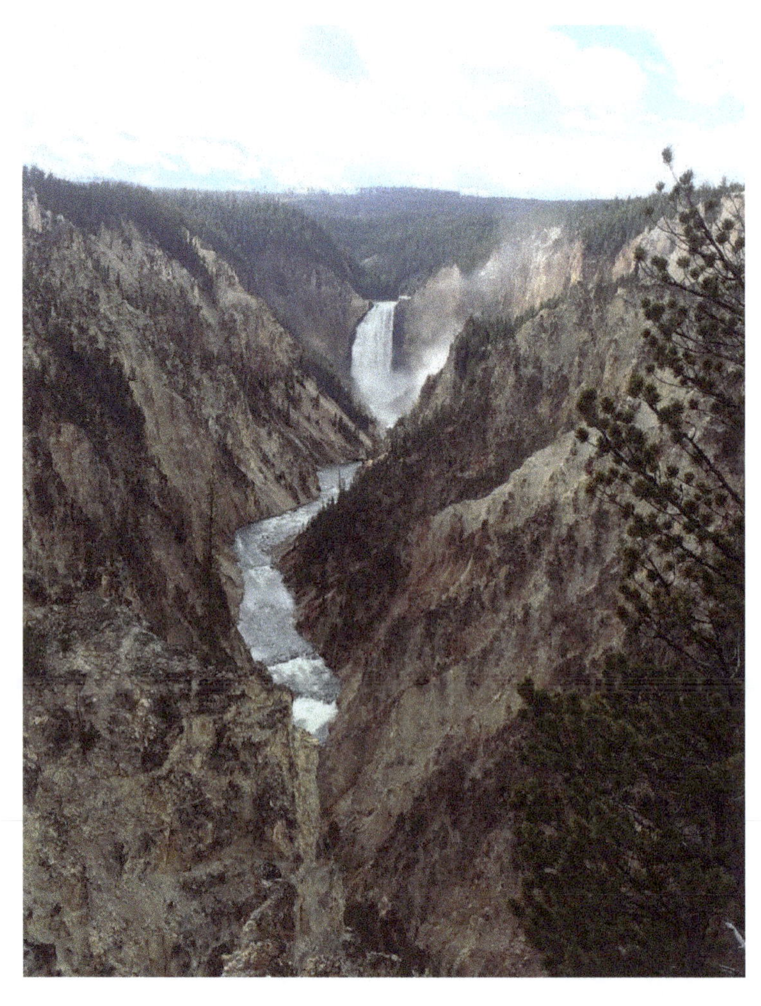

On Top of the Mountain

On top of the mountain,
Is where I will be.
I will live on top.
With God looking over me.

I will live my life.
For all to view,
And see You, my God,
And shout how I love You.

Guide me,
With your protecting hands.
Help me be ready!
For your promised land.

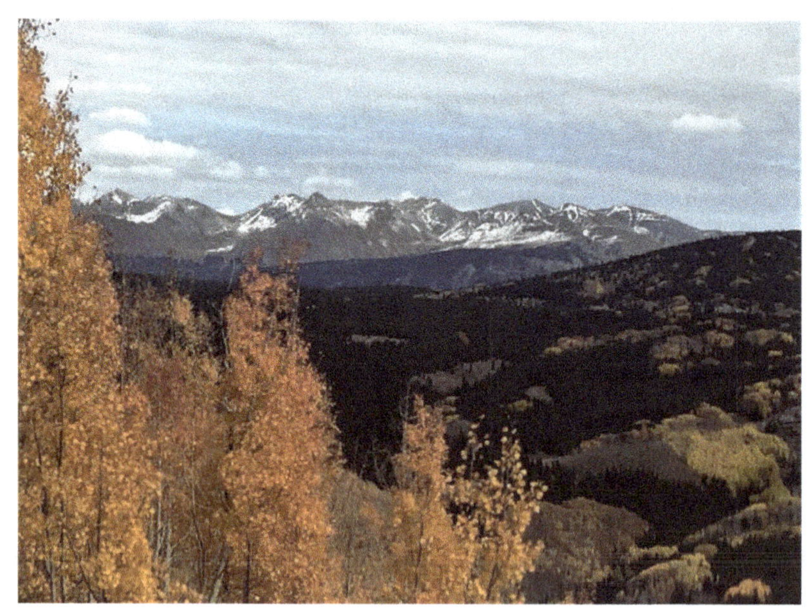

Your Creation

So simple and perfect is your creation,
From every angle we look.
I took my camera and then I searched,
Thinking I would put it all in a book.

As I got to the seaside, I saw your beauty.
I looked down the beach and beyond.
Then I saw all the pollution and was saddened.
What we have done to your creation is wrong.

I turned and went to the mountains,
And climbed up and down every range.
I searched the beauty then thought of our hearts,
And how we needed to change.

I went back home and looked out my window.
I could still see your creation there.
If we would only look past our sinfulness.
We'd see your beauty and You everywhere.

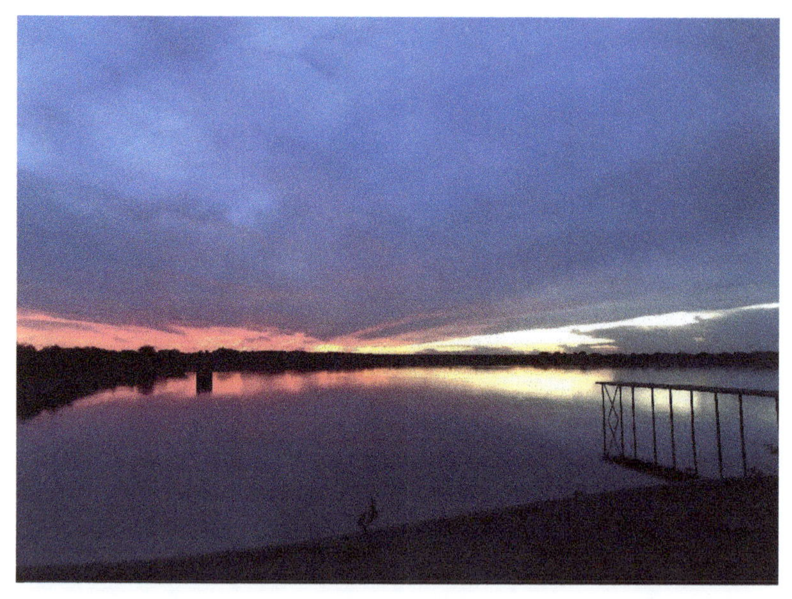

Speak To Me

Speak to me, my mighty King.
Tell me about your way.
I want to hear from you everything.
Guide my every day.

I hear the sound of your silent glory.
I long to hear it more.
It fills me with a calm and peace.
Like I've never known before.

Lord, guide us in this world of yours.
Please stop us, as it we destroy.
I ask you; I beg you, I plead with you!
Your love and mercy, I employ!

God, your perfect presence fills the air.
You are our mighty King!
You have the splendor above all else,
It is You who created everything.

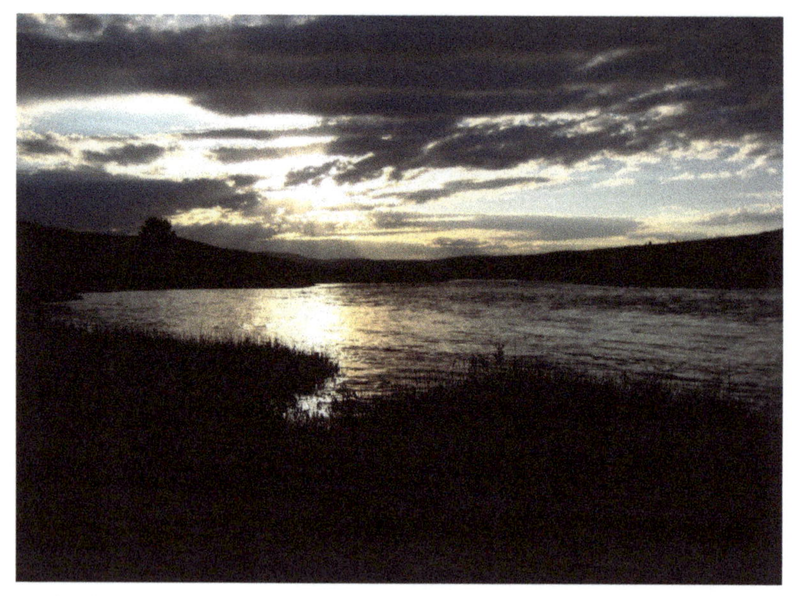

God Sees

When God looks down on this creation of His,
What do you think He sees?

Does He see rolling plains and blue skies?
Or the corruption from you and me?

What do we see when we look across,
Our country so vast and free?

Do we see growth, beauty, and God's grace,
All that He meant it to be.

Or do we see that growth and beauty,
As from us mistakenly?

Do we see His creation slowly sickened?
Do we see what God sees?

My prayer for God is to hopefully see,
Love from you and me.

My prayer to all people and my family,
Is to know all Jesus came to be.

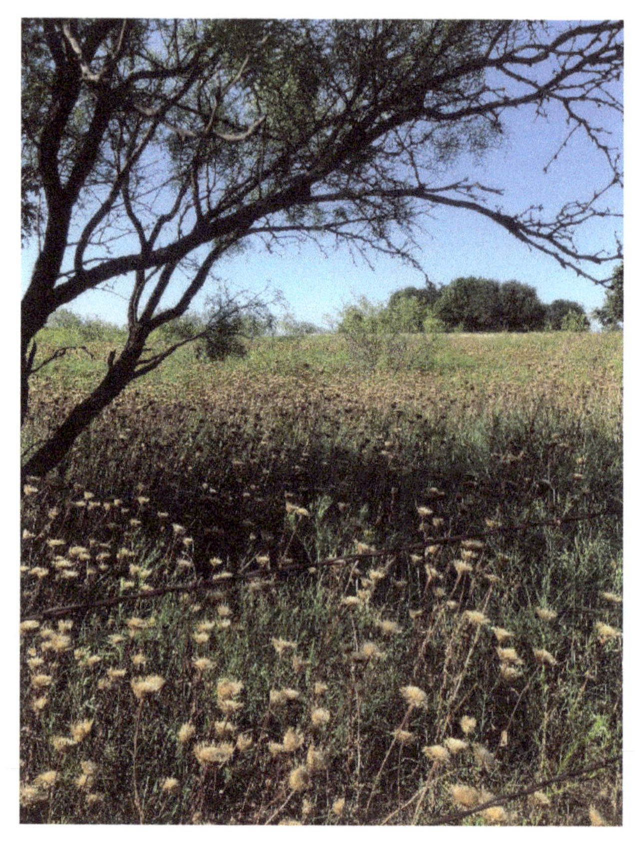

When I Die

When I die and leave this place,
It is time for me to go.
Don't cry, don't mourn, no sorrow for me.
You know why and to where I go.

I leave you with thoughts to ponder and yearn,
And the knowledge that I knew.
I leave you with love and support.
From a God that wants to know you.

Heed His call and listen hard.
React and for God be still.
Follow Jesus with all you do,
And the Holy Spirit's guidance you will feel.

I leave you with my heart.
And wisdom from God above.
My heart will never leave you.
And neither will my love.

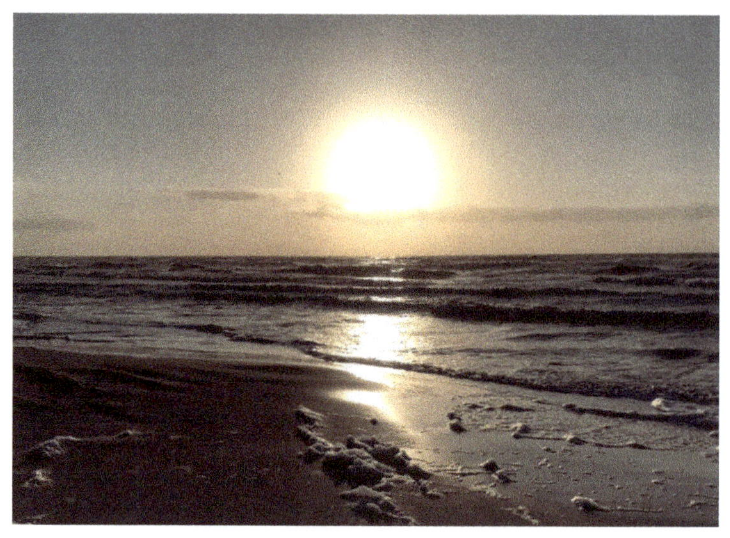

My Heart is That You Do Too

I have chosen to be cremated; my body need not remain. Why should it? It'd take up space and I'm not in it. I prefer my ashes to be scattered as I hope my testimony has been. I know cremation isn't for everyone, but sharing our testimony is.

I want no urn or sentimental vase. I want nothing left of me. My life is all for Jesus, and I hope to leave Him for you to see.

Please take my ashes to the ocean. Any ocean will do. To me, the ocean is a great place showing God's massiveness and vast beauty. You just let them go to blow in the wind. God will know what to do. He will take them where He wants them. That's all you need to do.

I hope you keep memories of me and think of them often but think of God so much more. In fact, think of Him all the time and me so much less than ever before.

And I hope your memories of me include my sharing His love for you. That's what is most important, and what I always hoped to do.

As you watch my ashes wash away in the waves, say a prayer of thanksgiving to Jesus and ask Him if you're saved. Please be sure God has His Holy Spirit in you. I will be singing praises to Him in heaven, and I hope to see you there, too.

So, there need be nothing left of me, no body, no treasures, and no legacy. Jesus is the one who was, is, and always will be. Him, God, and the Holy Spirit are here for eternity. I will leave my love for them first and then leave my love for you. My hope, my prayer, what's in my heart, is that you do too. Amen.

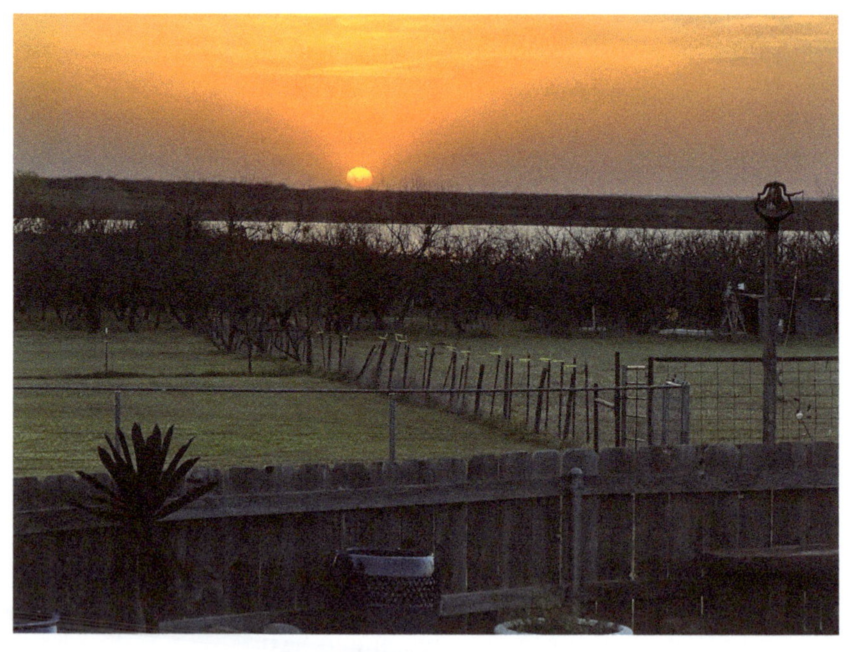

My Forgotten Prayer

I look out my window and see the beautiful landscape toward the lake. I wasn't always surrounded by beauty. When I was a little girl, my mother was tragically killed. After that I lived in different homes. I saw the evil side of this world I never knew existed. I prayed and begged God to give me back my safe, loving home but He didn't answer. At least, that's what I thought. This was a big prayer for a child. I have now lived in the same house for the past twenty plus years. I pray for others and wait to hear about their answers from God, because I remember that long forgotten childhood prayer of mine that I thought God never answered and I had stopped praying about.

I pray this way because one day as I was walking through my patio looking out toward the lake, I realized God did answer my long-forgotten childhood prayer! That prayer of having a safe, loving, home. It was all around me. God had never forgotten! That day I understood Psalm 37:4 about God giving us the desires of our heart if we take delight, hope, and seek Him. I now see how God answers our prayers, our desires, in the small things and small ways too. Things like that secure comfort of our homes, being able to pursue the creativity of our talents that too come from God and every color of everything we see like the landscape out my window that I see daily. God wants us to have enjoyment, to have the desires of our hearts, even the desires we've long forgotten. God wants to answer our every prayer. The signs of God are there. We just have to look. I hope you seek God and see how He wants to give you your desires. I know He gives me mine.

Family

We love because he first loved us
(1 John 4:19 ESV).

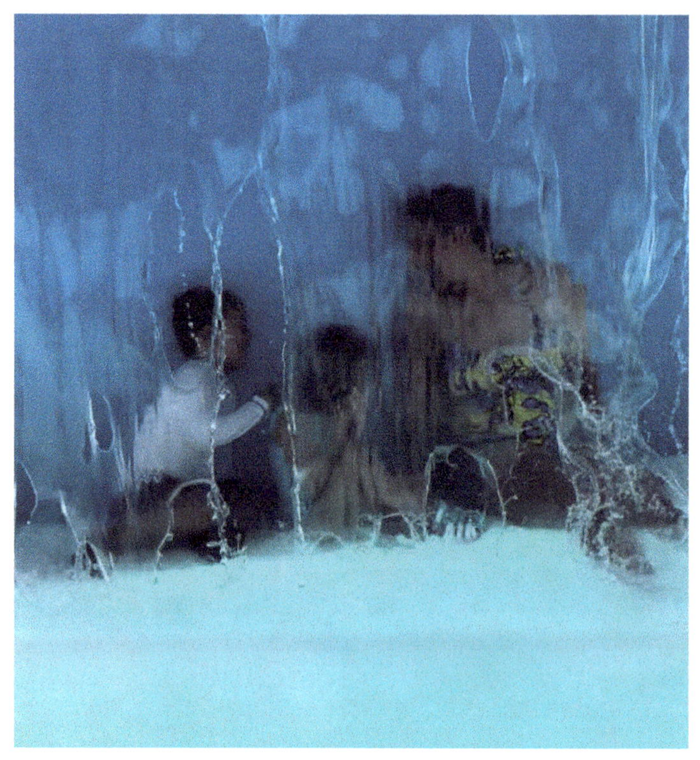

Childhood Memories

I remember going in the little car.
Avon bags in tow.
Just me, my mom, and brother,
Off to deliver we would go.

I remember them having me recite,
Numbers and ABC's as we went.
Even though I was not in school yet.
To them it was a day well spent.

I remember trying so hard to do a good job.
They loved me and I loved them.
I had no way of knowing,
How the future would be so dim.

My mom went first and met God in heaven.
My brother followed only a few years after.
The losses were so very hard on me.
It led to my life being a disaster.

With God I eventually came through it all.
I must give Him all the praise.
He led me, protected me, and gave me love.
And He will for all of my days.

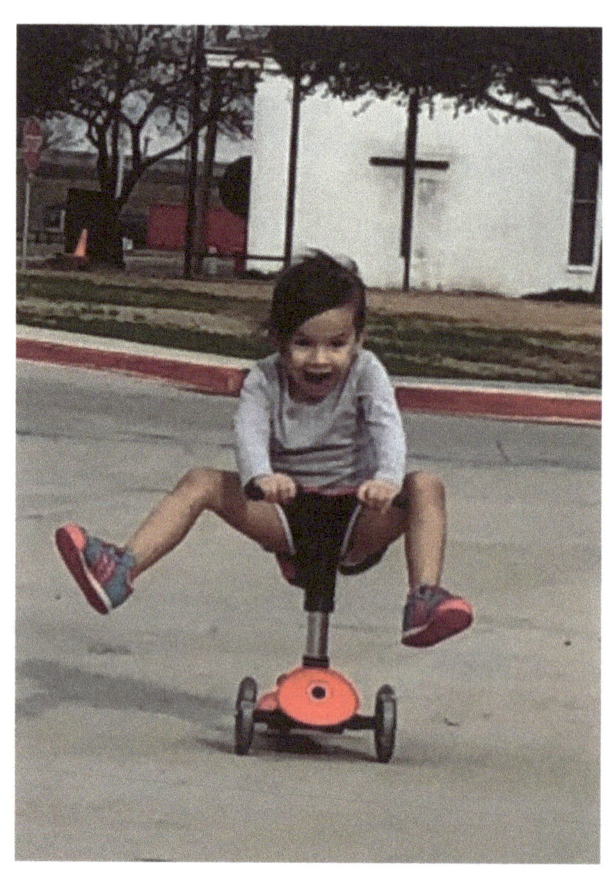

A First Bike

Remember your first bike?
The breeze on your face,
The wind in your hair.
Riding down the street,
You were the only one there.

Remember your first bike?
The falls,
The scraped knees.
Those happy, youthful, days,
Of childhood ease.

Remember your first bike?
I remember mine.
And I pass the memory down.
My child just got hers.
The memory goes around.

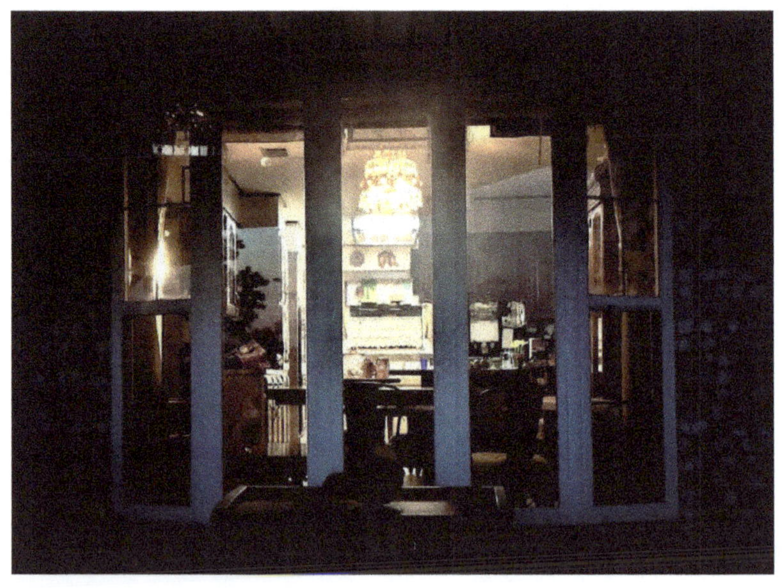

Muffled

Do you ever look at your world,
As from the outside in?
It gives a different view.
Things seem clearer,
More in perspective.
In a way, somewhat new.
When you muffle your surroundings,
And look through in a different light,
Try to visualize how things are inside.
When I do look, I see cozy warmth.
That God is able to provide.
As the view is muffled,
When I look as from the outside in,
I see my family and our life together unfold.
I want to be ready for them.
Always ready to hug and hold.
And to wrap them in my arms,
To muffle any evil outside sound.
I want to protect their lives.
But I know I can't.
I can only pray we're all heaven bound.

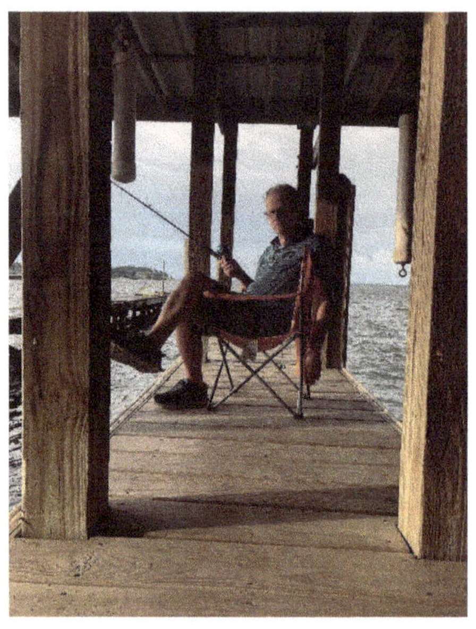

Happy Birthday, Jim!

To my husband, to my spouse,
the King of our building, lawn mower, and house.
I never was one to give you any "honey dos."
But I never missed a chance to say, "I love You!"
You're the best husband that could ever be,
Because you've always put up with me!
I watch you mow, then sit and read.
And I know you're the only one I'll ever need!
You're my husband, my provider, the one I love.
I know you're my blessing from up above!
So, know today, tomorrow, as every day before,
That I will love you more and more!

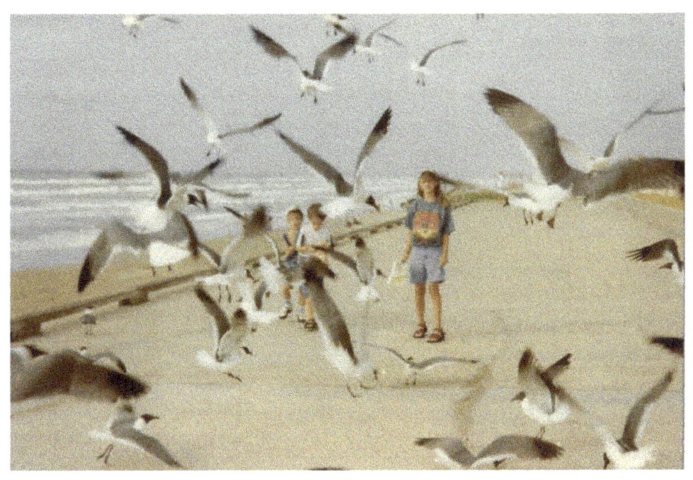

A Little Girl

There once was a sweet little girl,
Who had lots of hair but no curls.
She would run, skip, and jump really high,
And laugh and sing the whole day by.

She's almost grown.
And will soon be on her own.
With her life starting,
She'll one day be parting.

We'll remember her always,
As that same little one,
Who only wanted,
To spend the day having fun.

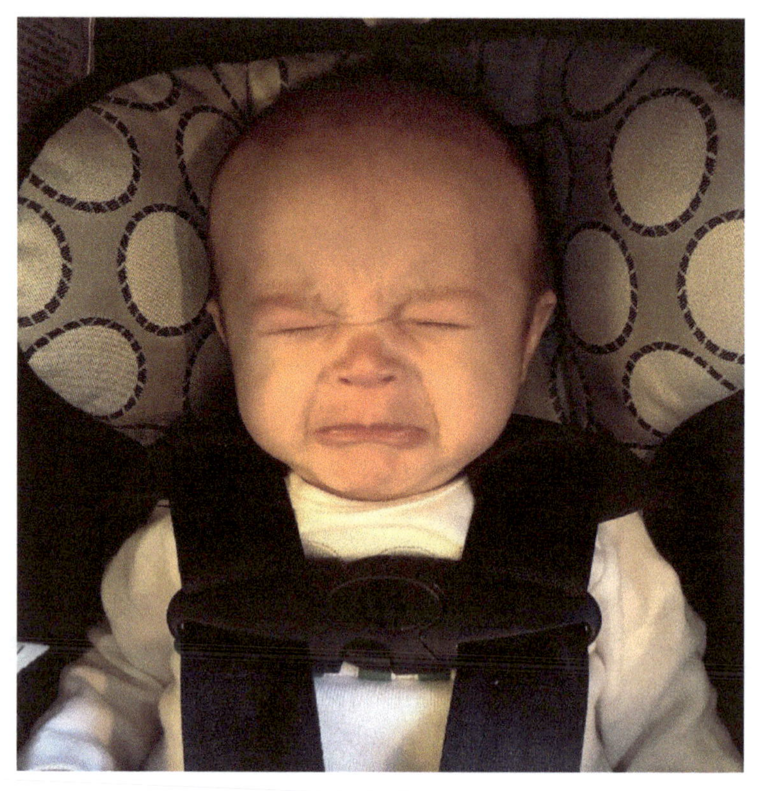

My Son

My son was always crying.
And it made his mother feel sad.
It wasn't because he was hurt.
And he wasn't even mad.

He just seemed to be that way.
There was sadness in his heart.
It wasn't because he didn't understand.
He was kind and very smart.

So why was my son always crying,
And would it ever end?
One day he'd know the reason.
And cheerfulness would begin.

He cried because he had a tender heart.
And mourned as in Matthew 5:4.
But God would come and comfort him.
For now, and evermore.

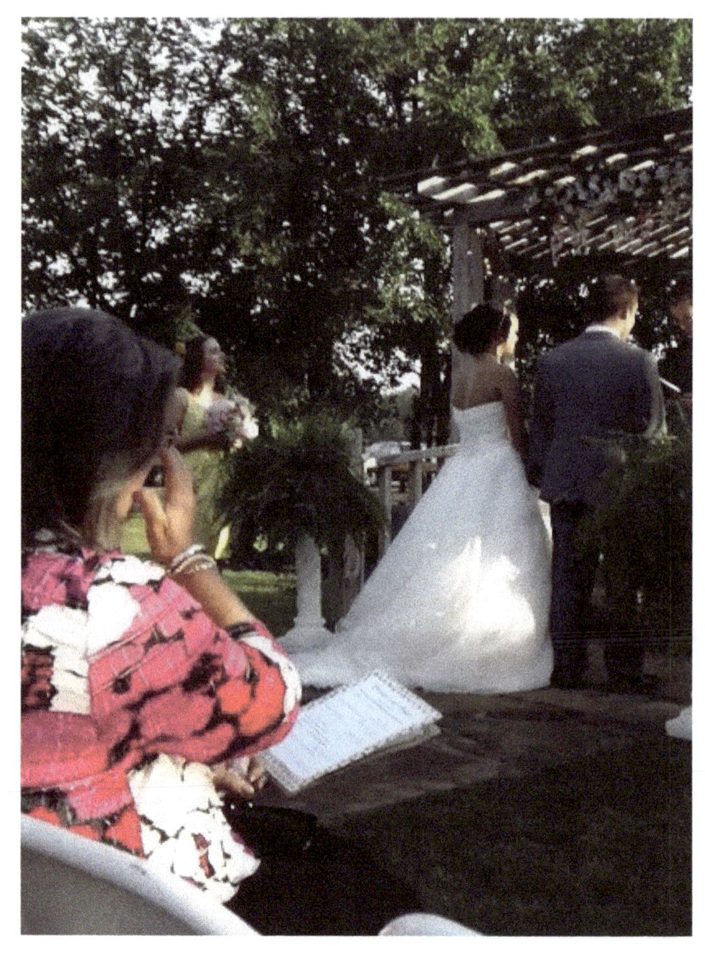

A Mom's Discourse

How do I prepare the way?
I knew that you would leave one day.
To follow another in love so true.
I'm happy about it but I still feel blue.

To know that in this whirlwind of life,
Instead of me, you'll go to your wife.
You'll go for love, advice, and for safety.
My time is done, you're no longer my baby.

I'll learn to live without you in my arms.
Don't let my discourse cause you alarm.
I know my time has gone away.
And now with her, your loyalty must stay.

Be calm my son,
Your life has just begun.
She's perfect, that I can see.
And I know you will both be so happy.

One more thing as you move along.
Please listen to my words and don't get me wrong.
But as your mom who held you so long ago,
I'll love you forever, that you must know.

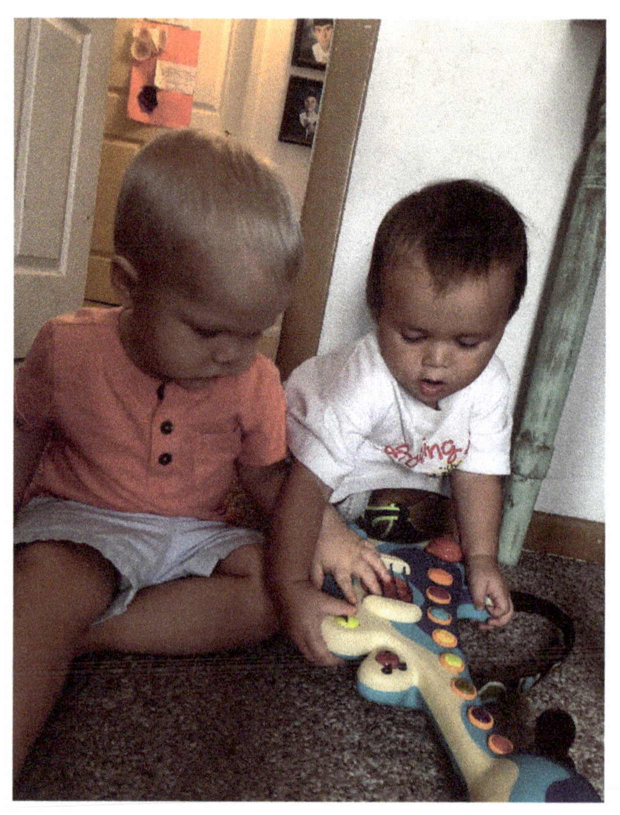

This Son of Mine

And his mercy is for those who fear him
from generation to generation
(Luke 1:50 ESV).

This son of mine has a new son.
And my other son has one too.
My sons were close growing up,
All the while learning so much new.

They eventually moved into their own homes.
Their paths went different ways.
But even with new sons and family,
They would still be close every day.

These sons of mine are blessings to me.
And now their sons are also.
Just three months apart, close cousins they'll be.
And hopefully Jesus they'll know.

Jesus and John the Baptist were cousins, too.
They were close and born six months apart.
My wish for mine is that they're always close.
And will love each other with all of their hearts.

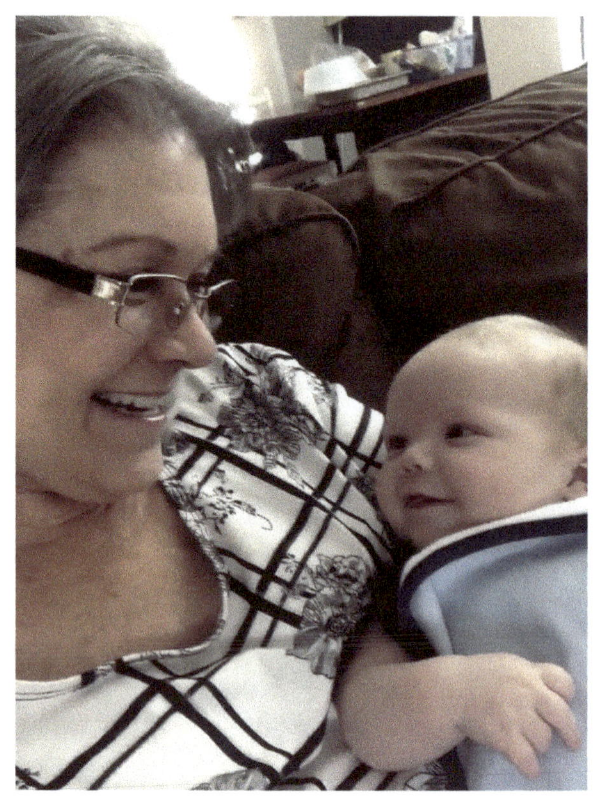

My Grandson

This baby in my arms,
Means the world to me.
Not only is he my grandson,
But he's my baby's baby.
My baby who was once in my arms,
My last to hold so tenderly.
Before the growing up started,
And a man he came to be.

This baby in my arms,
Will not stay this way for long.
He will grow so very quickly.
I pray for him to be strong.
Not just strong in strength,
But strong in every way.
In physical, mental, and spiritual,
God, guide him every day.

I pray for his Daddy, also.
And his Mama, too.
Thank you, Lord God!
For these wonderful gifts from you!

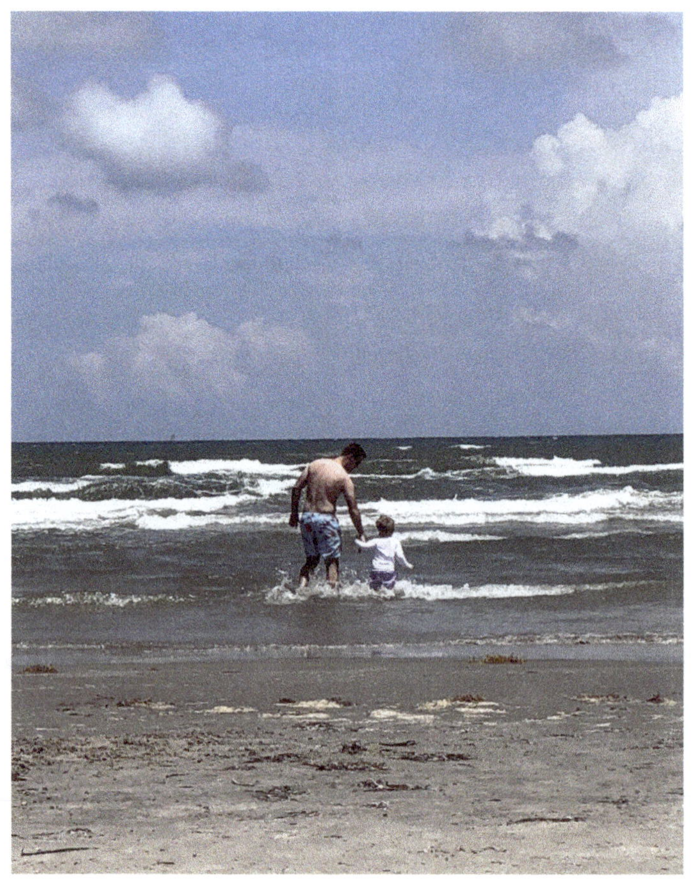

In a Different Way

He'll never teach you football.
Or how in basketball to score.
But he will teach you something else.
That means so much more.
I know it hurt his heart,
Because at first you didn't respond.
But then you turned around,
And the two of you started to bond.
You showed us all a way of life,
Through another open door.
We love you to the moon and back.
With your Daddy's love so much more.
We wouldn't want to change you.
God made you different in a special way.
And as you grow, we grow too.
And love you more each day!

I dedicate this poem to all those parents who have
children that God made perfect in a different way.

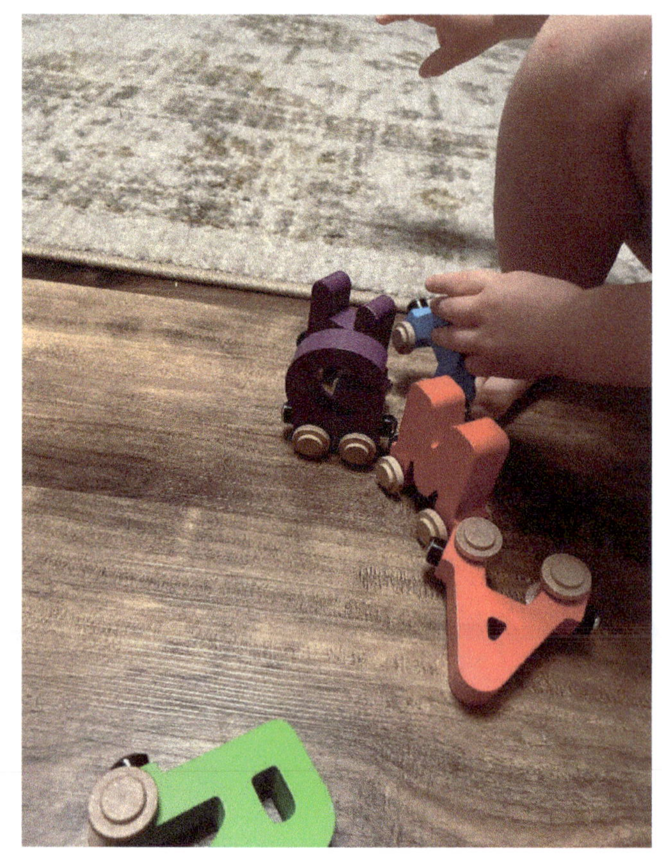

Destination Interrupted

He says, I don't have to stop.
And play with you.
I'm doing just fine.
I know what to do.
And when the occasion,
Does come around,
I'll take you by the hand.
For us to explore all I've found.
We can have our fun together.
And put our words aside.
Words can take too much time.
Come on. I'll be your guide.
I can take you to my world.
Where I like it quiet and calm.
Listen, there's so much to be doing.
You'll find it's a place to belong.
And then you'll understand,
How I can say I'm doing fine.
You just need to sit and see.
This special world of mine.

Any child with special needs is a destination
interrupted but it's a special interruption with a
beautiful outcome. Please take the time to notice and
admire. There are amazing things going on in these
worlds!

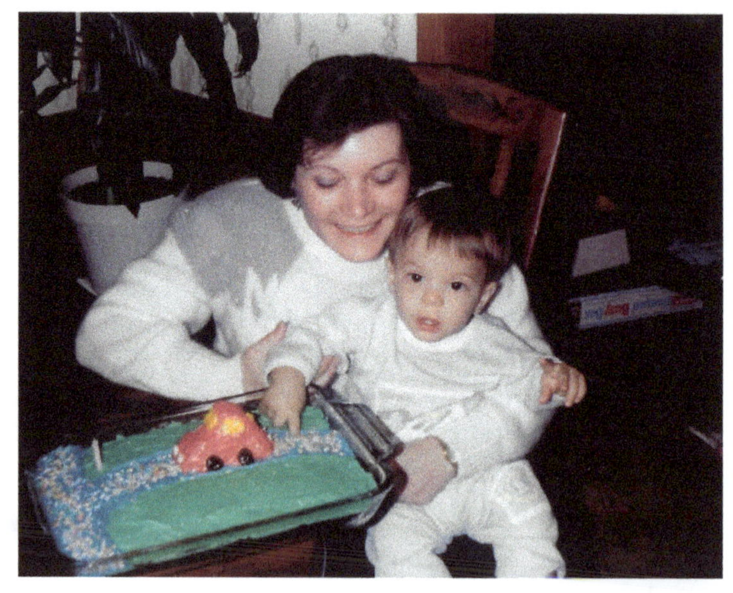

You Are My Gift

I don't know what I could give you,
That would show how precious you are to me.
You are my baby, my heart in my arms,
You are so valuable,
More than I ever thought could be.

I don't have enough wealth,
To show you how much I care.
You mean more than anything.
And the depth of my love for you,
I know you're unaware.

You are my baby, my heart, my life.
I will love you till the end of time.
You are a special blessing from God,
That He gave to always be mine.

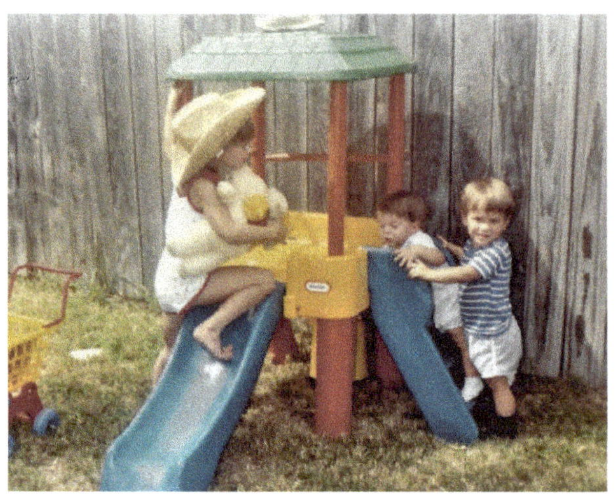

My Babies

If I forget to ask how you are,
It's not because I do not care.
My older mind is thinking of all I want to ask.
And it just may not think to go there.

If I forget to tell you,
Stories of you when you were small.
It's not because I don't treasure them.
It is definitely not that at all.

I love you now as always.
My babies you'll always be.
And if I forget to tell you,
You're always in my heart, that I guarantee!

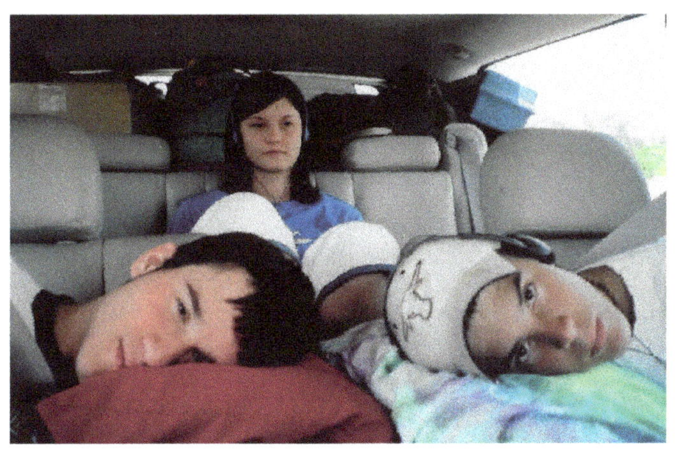

Never perfect

As I was raising my kids, they had a very imperfect person trying to give them a perfect life. When all they needed was for me to be real.

I am not a perfect mom.
I never hope to be.
But even though I am not,
My love for you is totally.
I make mistakes.
I say things wrong.
But my desire for your life
Is perfectly, unendingly, strong.
So, my children always remember,
And forever always know,
I'm not perfect and neither are you.
But I love you, even though.

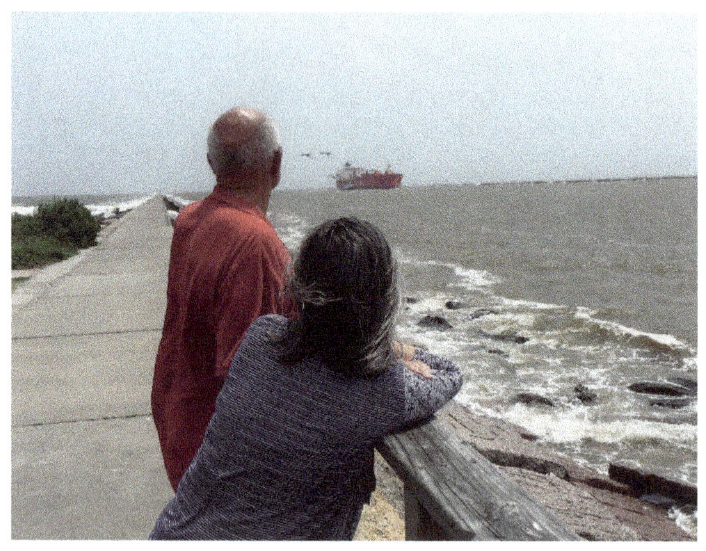

My Daddy Forever
You'll Be

Sitting beside his hospital bed,
Makes me want to weep.
I think of all the memories,
And the promises we didn't keep.

The memories weren't all good.
We had times that shouldn't be.
But he knew I loved him.
And I knew he loved me.

There was one last thing that he said to me,
In that one moment he knew who I was,
Blurting it out he said, "I love you!"
Then went back to calling me "Cous."

I love you, Daddy, I always will.
My Daddy, forever you'll be.
I hope and pray I'll see you again,
For always, in eternity.

The memories weren't always good.
But they were ours and that's why I weep.
They are dear and deep in my heart,
And there they will forever keep.

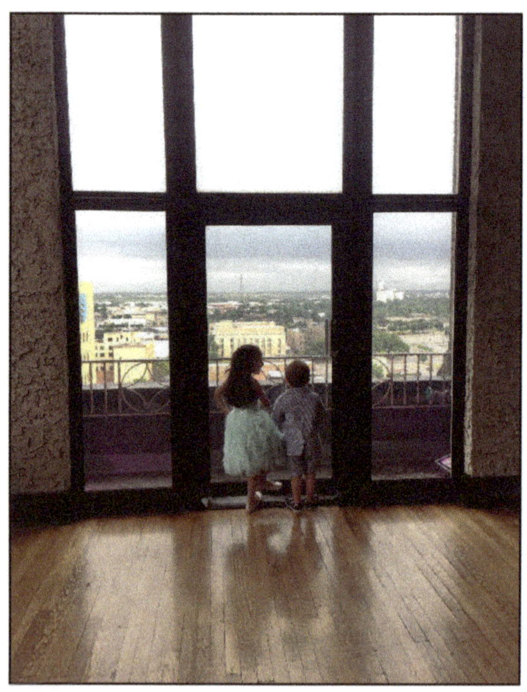

To My Children and All Children

A child is special, a child is dear.
I hold my children in my heart very near.
For all you parents and parents to be,
God's Word is precious everlastingly.

So, teach your children kindness, teach them love.
Teach them to know our Heavenly Father above.
Teach every child to know in their heart,
About following Jesus, and that He can't be bought.

Life

Fear not, for I am with you; be not dismayed, for I am your God; I will strengthen you, I will help you, I will uphold you with my righteous right hand (Isaiah 41:10 ESV).

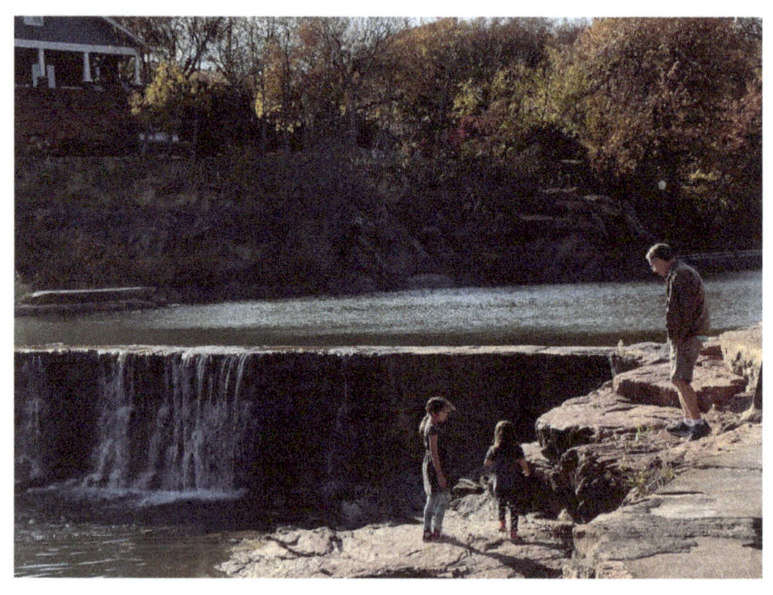

The Days Before

Party lines,
Fives and dimes,
Lots of time,
To play.
Black and white,
Or no TV
Don't you see?
That's how it used to be,
Back in my childhood days.
You play all day.
Sleep well at night.
Life was simple.
And it was alright.
Thoughts of the future,
Were not there.
But that's ok,
Love was everywhere.
Back in my childhood days.

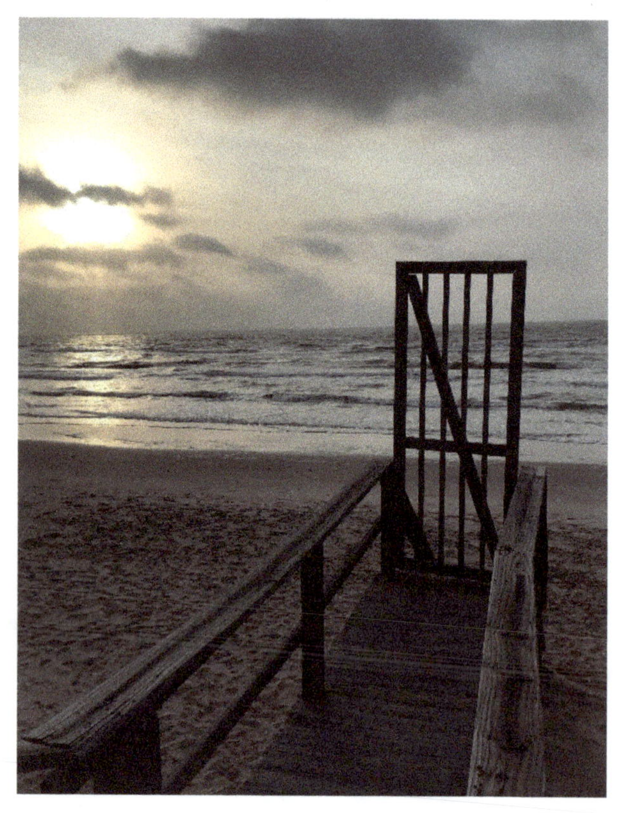

The Ties That Bind

The ties that bind.
Are lifted now.
They hold me tight no more.

The ties that bound.
Me to my past,
Are now behind the door.

I've closed that door.
To never enter again.
I don't want life as it was before.

I've lifted the ties,
To be free from sin,
And see what the future has in store.

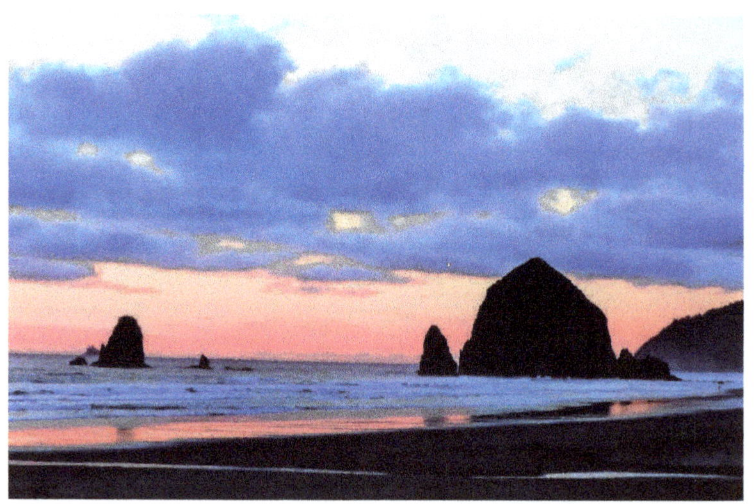

Emotions

Serenity; calm, soothing,
Peaceful serenity.

Vigilance; harmful, hateful,
Destructive vigilance.

Love; life, family,
Forever love.

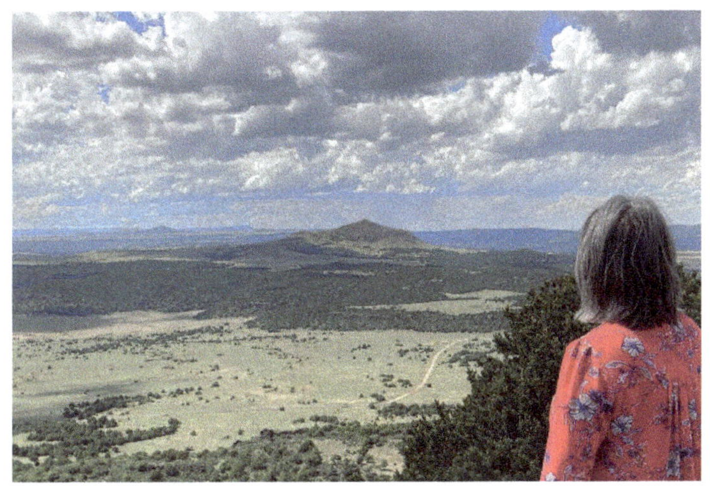

In My Rush

In my rush I missed the time,
The time to listen and be still.
In my rush I missed the time,
The time to pray and kneel.

In my rush I missed the time,
The time to show you my love.
In my rush I missed the time,
The time to see your glory from above.

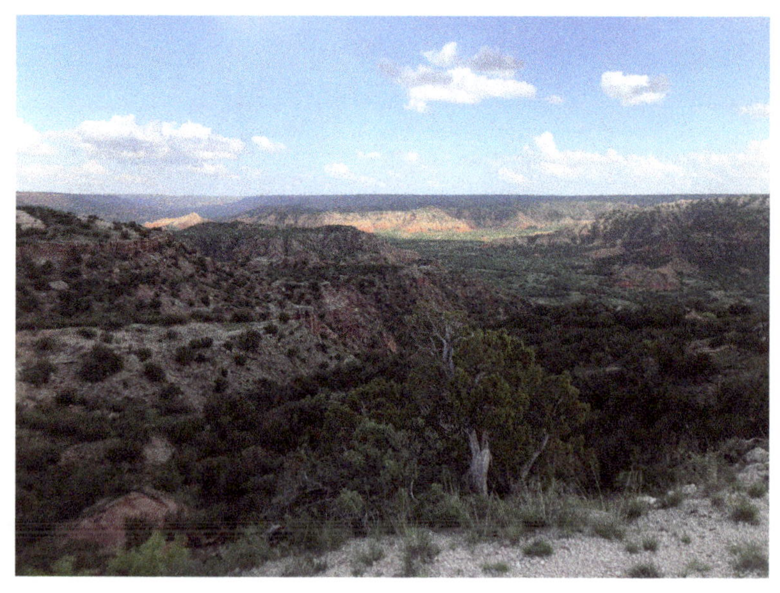

Written for You

What kind of day do you hope to find?
Happy and bright or blue.
Do you know from where the day comes?
God made it just for you.

I hope you think of good things,
Happy and bright things too.
All my days will be in thoughts,
Happy and bright for you.

Long ago there was a time.
When for me sad thoughts prevailed.
Fighting against thinking these thoughts,
Will help us all be well.

I wish you joy, I wish you laughs,
And I wish you all the more.
Remember this was written for you,
And my prayers came before.

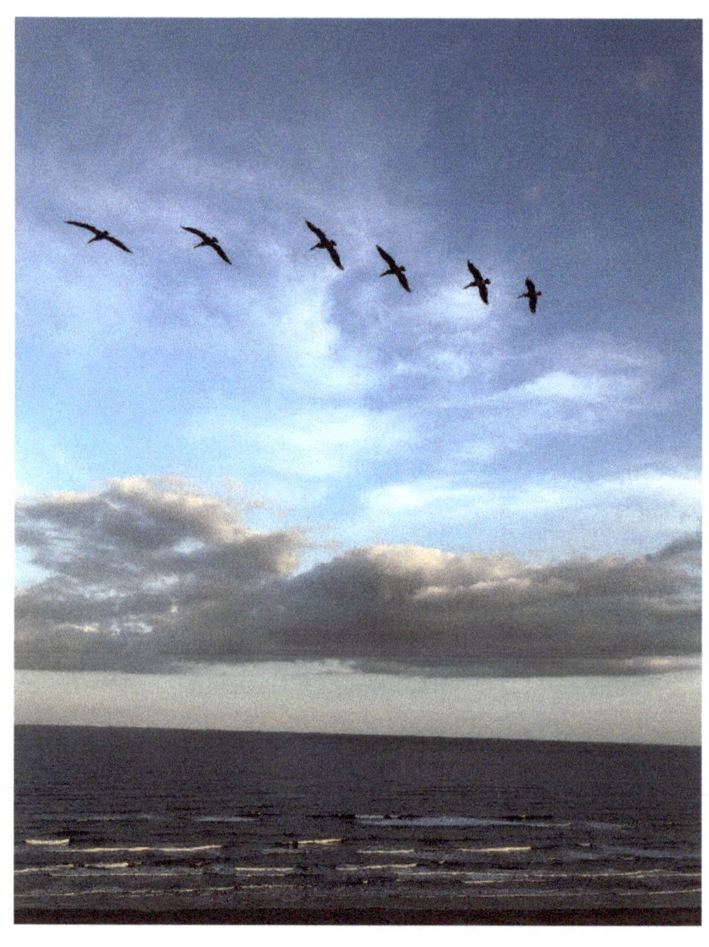

I See the Birds

I see the birds flying over the ocean.
They look so peaceful as they soar.
The Bible tells us God cares for them.
And He loves us so much more.
I see the trees lose their leaves,
Only to come back in the spring.
We see so many colors through them.
It's one more reason to praise our King.
I see the ladybug ever so sweetly,
And so quickly whisking by.
In all my 59 years on earth,
I had forgotten they could fly.
We see the deer running and playing.
And so gracefully jump to the next pasture.
Psalm 148 tells us even these creatures,
Know to praise our Lord and Master.
So as each day comes to an end,
And the sun starts to set,
I'll remember I praised Him all day long.
And for each day I will have no regret.

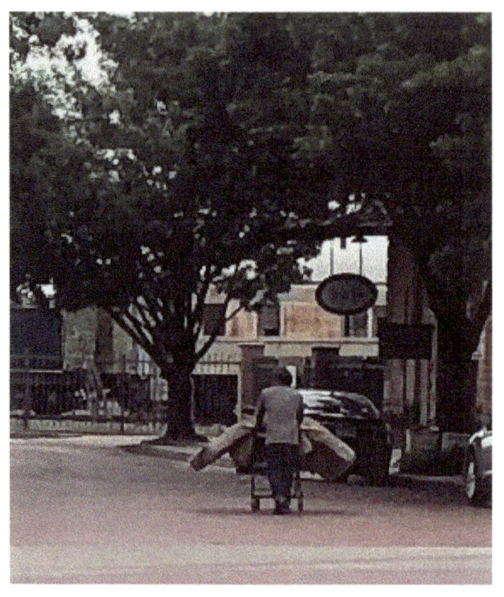

*How
Many
Miles?*

It saddens me to see a man.
Standing on the side of the road.
To know he's been there all night.
And has nowhere to go.
He stands and waits,
Not knowing what to do next.
What the day will give?
Will it be work or rest.
Help him know your eternal home,
And that you're our great Yahwey,
I lift him to you through Jesus,
Our to You, forever highway!

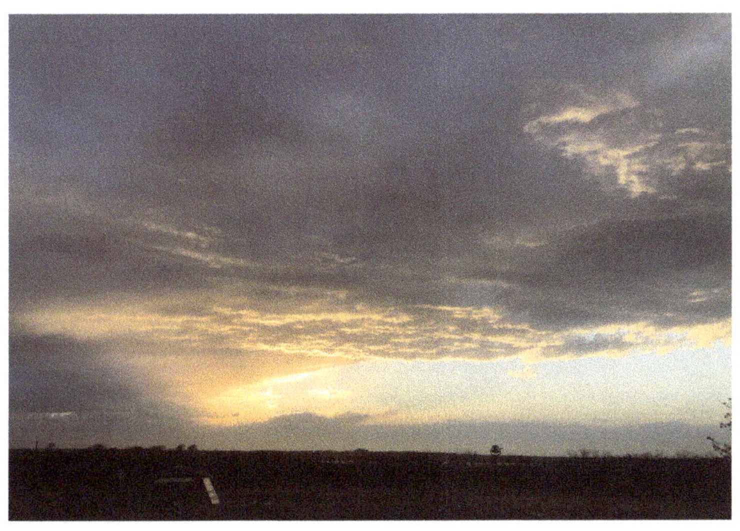

The Daze of Grief

And after you have suffered a little while, the God of all grace, who has called you to his eternal glory in Christ, will himself restore, confirm, strengthen, and establish you (1 Peter 5:10 ESV).

I know that feeling,
Of sadness and gloom.
The wrenching desire,
To wake up soon.
I hope this nightmare is not for real.
I pray to God, and wait, being real still.
The daze that comes never leaves,
To those of us while we grieve.

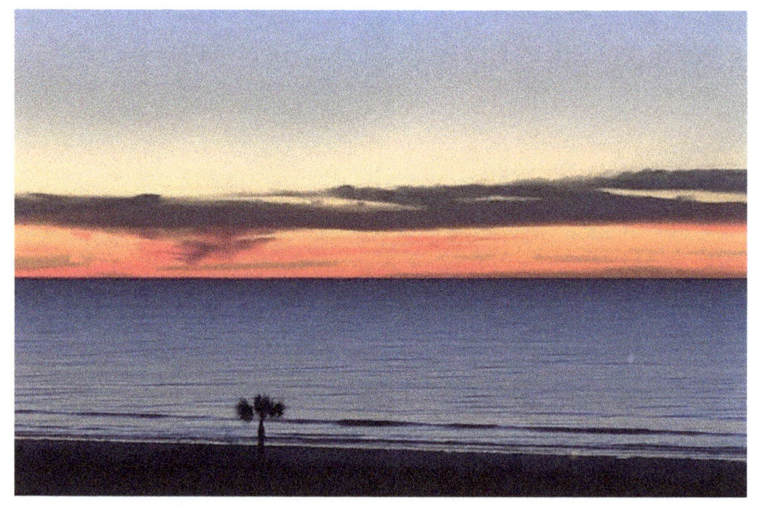

When the Waves
are Calm

When the waves are calm,
It stills my heart.
I know that you are here.

When the calm wind blows,
From end to start,
I feel your presence near.

When I sit and listen,
I know we'll never part.
And there's nothing for me to fear.

When the waves are calm,
It fills my heart.
I have the strength to persevere.

You calm my soul,
With your creation's art,
And have made your love so clear.

From sharing your word,
I will not depart.
And I hope and pray all hear.

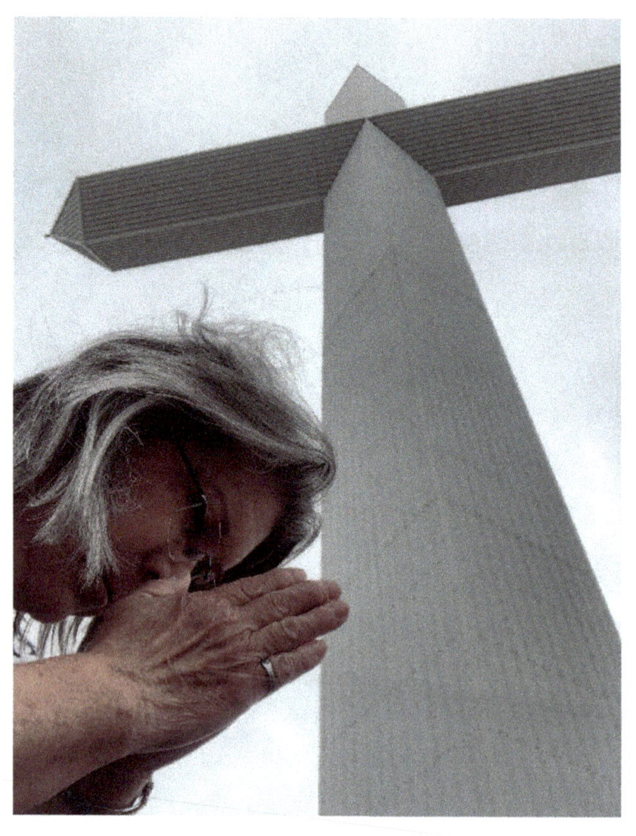

My Thoughts About Forgiveness

Everyone wants closure when they go through a crime, especially one unsolved. My closure came through forgiveness. It could only come from forgiveness.

It's not about life, it's not about death, it's about what we do in between. The true story of my family's fifty-year-old unsolved murders gives light to what we do in between life and death. With the murders now *Unraveled, It's Time to Forgive.*

When you think the sky is falling,
Look toward forgiveness.

When it feels like the water is too deep,
Dive into forgiveness.

When your life seems to be on hold,
Reach out and take a stand with forgiveness.

Jesus hung on the cross,
For us to have forgiveness.

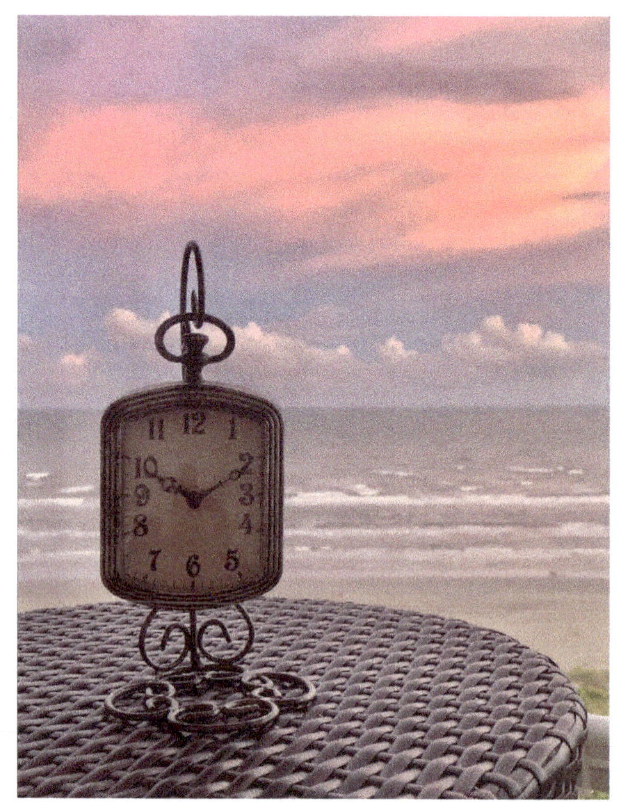

Tick Tock

Tick tock, tick tock,
Goes the clock.
Around and around,
Making that sound.
It doesn't slow,
For us to know,
The end won't stop.
Tick tock, tick tock.
We'll reach the end.
Something new will begin.
It does draw near.
That part is clear.
I'm ready now.
For me to go, somehow.
As I watch the clock.
Tick tock, tick tock.

Paul said it best, *"For to me to live is Christ, and to die is gain" (Philippians 1:21 ESV).*

I can only try to be ready as my life on earth ticks away toward heaven.

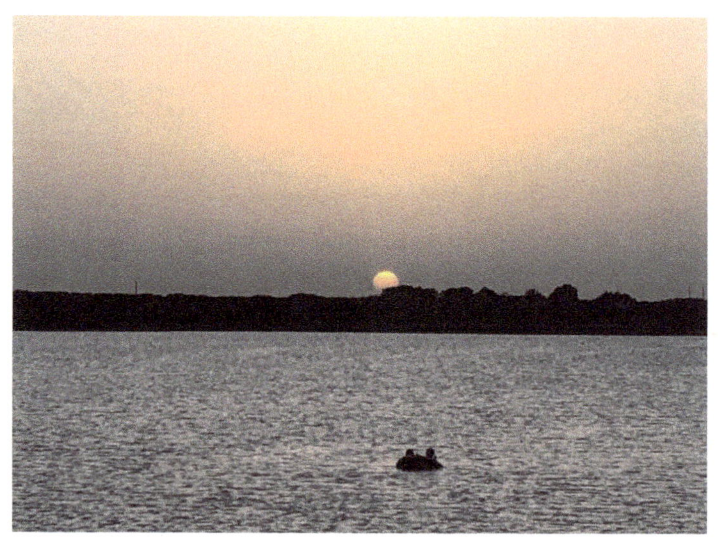

*The Change
I Wouldn't Need*

Do you ever wonder what would be?
If you could change your past?
Things would be so different for me,
But God still gave me happiness to last.

My life now is in a stronger mode,
Because of what happened as a child.
I would've stayed in that same sad abode,
But God looked down on me and smiled.

He knew I needed His help.
And, also, His guidance galore.
He knew the hurt and pain I felt,
And He loved me all the more.

So, if I could change what happened to me,
I'd instead give glory and praise to my King.
And from every moment I would not flee.
Because if I could, I would not change a thing.

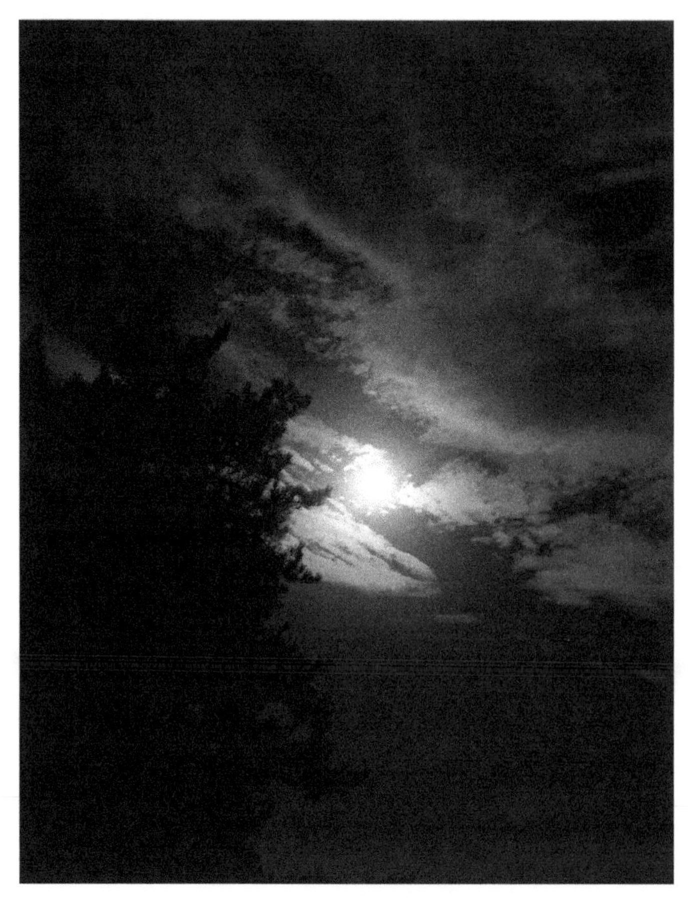

Melancholy

When you feel you have melancholy,
What do you do?
Do you seek a happy spot,
Or someone to talk to?
Do you sit and let it grow,
Do you sit and dwell?
It's a feeling we all know.
And I know it oh so well.
When you're feeling melancholy,
It's best to seek our Lord, Yahweh.
He'll show you peace and happiness.
He'll help you through your days.
We all have times of melancholy.
Days we're down or sad.
Or maybe it's thinking of something,
That happened that was bad.
But it's best to seek our Lord, Adonai.
When those times and memories hit.
He'll change our hearts to joy,
And make the sad memories quit.
🎵Praise Him, praise Him,
All ye little children.
God is love. God is love.🎵

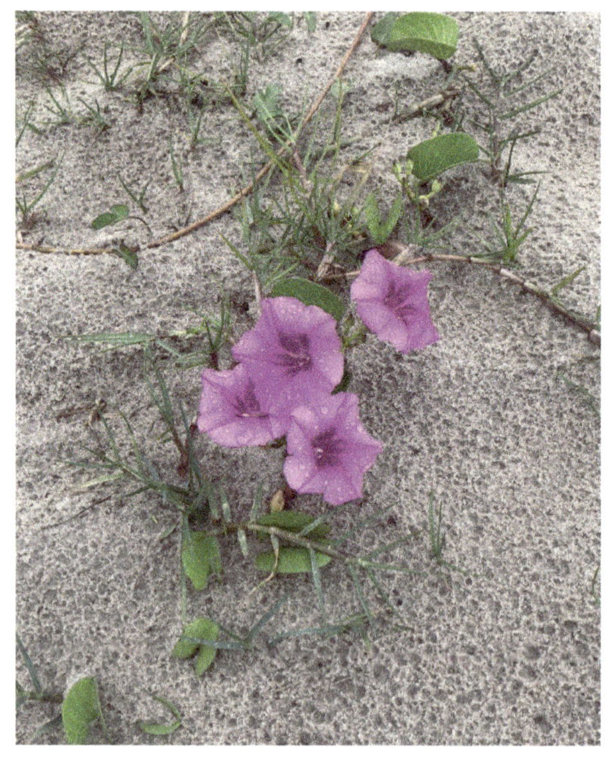

The Morning Glories
are Out in the Evening

Time is off.
Days seem wrong.
The morning glories are out in the evening.
From dusk to dawn,
I'm moving on.
I'm listening to the off world speaking.
I hear it now.
I'm not sure how.
With all the wrongness reaping.
Help us, Lord.
Guide our ways.
The morning glories are out in the evening.

The morning glories are a symbol of our time on earth, only open for a short time. They stand for rebirth and renewal. God promises and provides this to us. Unfortunately, we don't always see it.

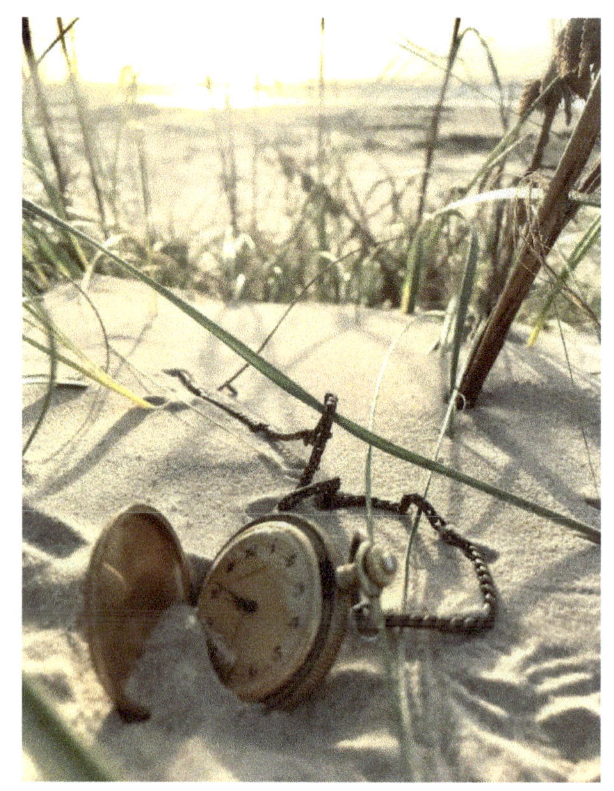

Time

Time has forgotten.
How much you did.

Time has forgotten.
How much you loved.

Time has forgotten.
How much you cared.

For all the time,
You were with me,

Your love grew.
So, my love grew.

Time may have forgotten.
But I never did.

Who do you need?
To remind of your love.

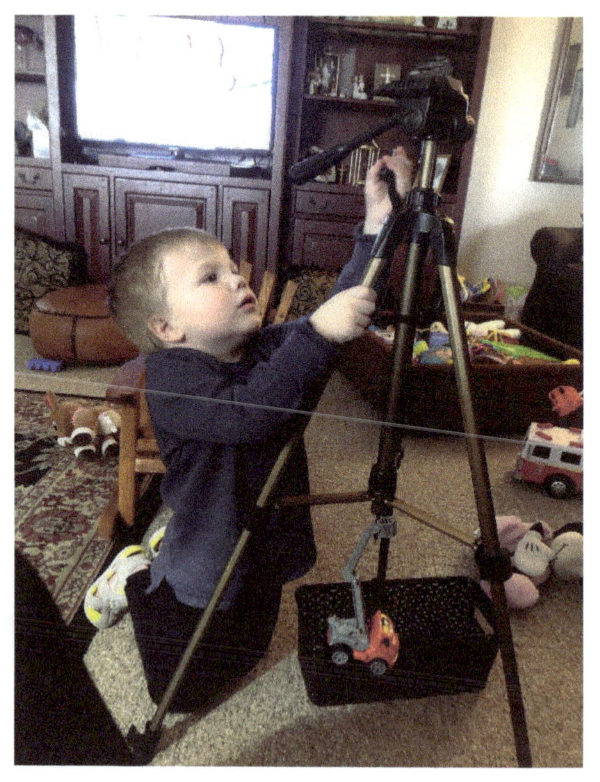

Never Say

Never say to someone about a child in front of that
child, "He's different."
We're all different.

Never say to someone in front of that child,
"He does things differently."
We all do things differently.

Never say in front of that child or to him,
"You aren't able to do that."
Are you unable to do something if you try?

A child grows up to think negative or positive
thoughts about themselves according to how
they are taught.
What do you think of yourself?

What do you want that child to think?

It's ok if he doesn't want to play right now.

It's ok. He's just doing things his own way, like we
all do.

All children are unique, special, and capable of
doing whatever they set their minds on.
I'm so thankful God made me and you that way too.

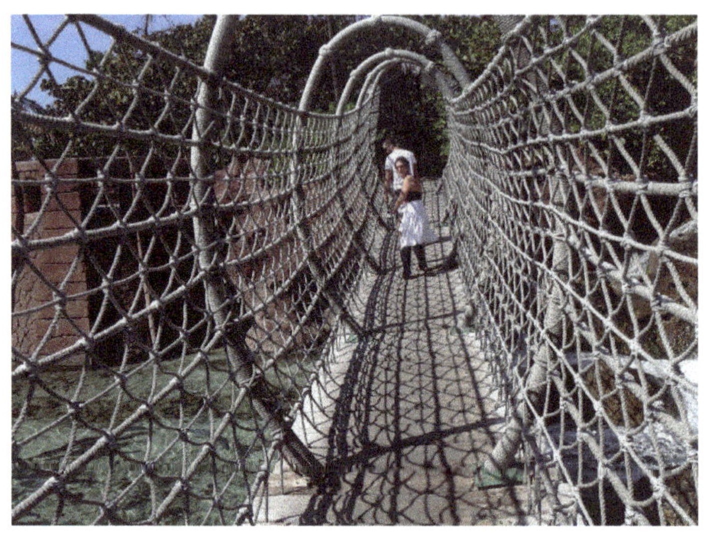

Climb

To the top.
Don't stop,
Climb, climb, climb.
To the bottom,
We go.
Slow, slow, slow.
All around,
And back again.
Through the depths,
Our soul to mend.
Which way to go?
We will know.
Climb, climb, climb.

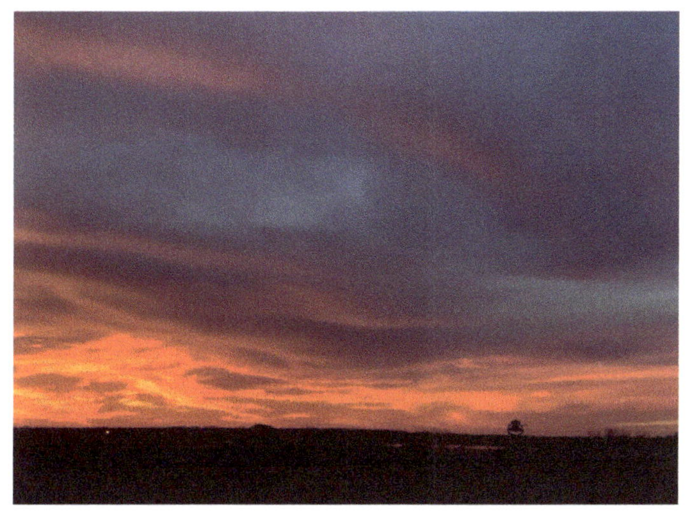

See the Beauty

Sometimes it's hard.
To see the beauty.
We sit and look and stare.
We wonder where.
The beauty went.
We simply don't see it there.
I wonder when.
The beauty stopped.
That was within our heart.
That's where the beauty.
Was first found.
And where it first,
Started to depart.

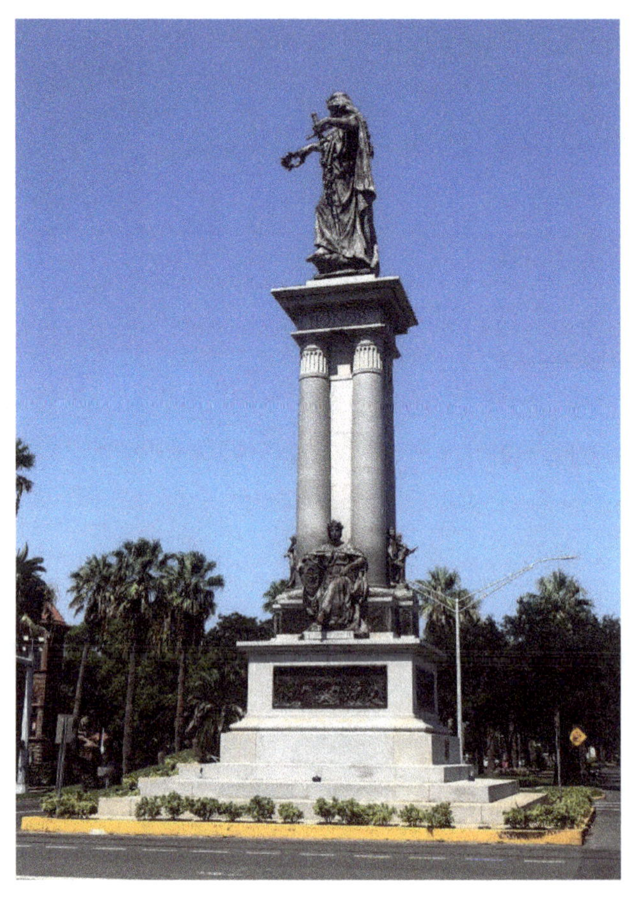

History

Please don't change our history.
It's detrimental if you do.
Make it accurate, add what's missing,
This will make the story through and through.

Please don't take away our statutes,
Of silver, bronze, metal, and gold.
Each of these have a purpose,
For our future generations to behold.

History is not all perfect.
There are flaws because of our hearts.
But this is how we learn and grow,
We need these old stories for a start.

So please don't take away history.
Whether happy or sad as it may be.
We must keep telling the stories,
Of every one of our nationalities.

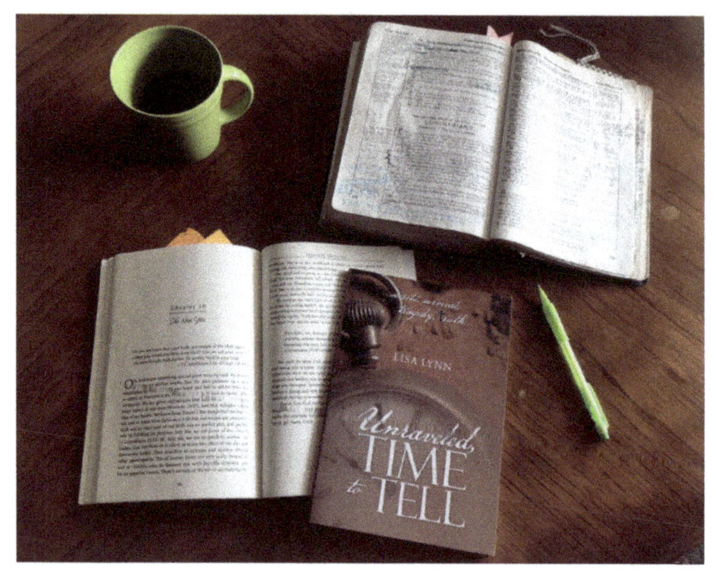

The Beauty of My Youth

More life poems can be found in chapter 13 and throughout my book, *Unraveled, Time to Tell."*

I think of myself as old and presentable.
I don't have the beauty as when I was young.
I remember the clothes, shoes, and the makeup.
Those days are past, older days have begun.

I remember my grandmas; will I be the same?
Will I have their habits of old age?
I wonder if I will take these habits gracefully,
Or if I will take them and feel disengaged.

Will I have the walking slower, sitting longer,
And having to think before all that I do.
These sound like things I should have always done.
Instead of just now be going through.

It's funny how now some things seem hard.
Simple things like touching my toes.
I know it's hard for the young to understand,
But everyone my age and older knows.

I won't grow old gracefully.
This is something I've always said.
But I think that is a saying,
I definitely need to get out of my head.

These older years are not really that bad.
It's a part of the cycle of life.
And I have no choice but to accept it,
And enjoy it without struggle or strife.

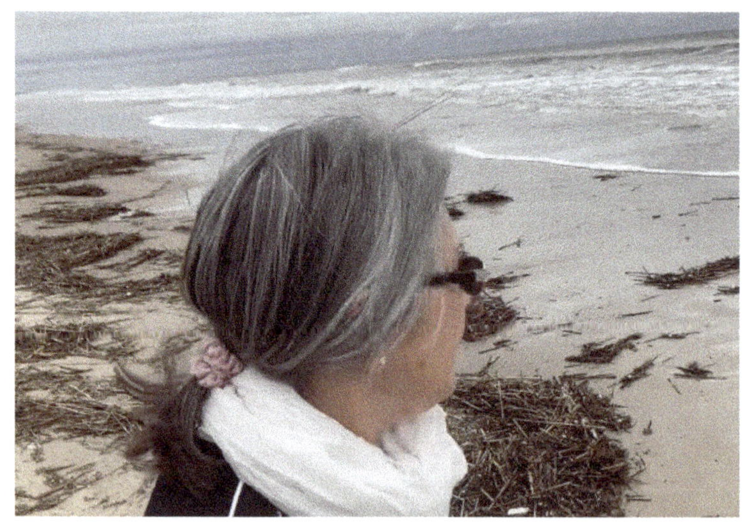

Gray on Black

Gray hair is a crown of glory; it is gained in a righteous life (Proverbs 16:31 ESV).

I found a few more grays today.
And my skin has started to creep.
But beauty is on the inside,
It's in your heart way down deep.

There is no need to worry,
No need to cry or care.
The Bible says gray is a sign of wisdom.
So, there is no need for despair.

And I cannot stop the time from coming,
Day after day after day.
I'm thankful for each and every one.
So thankful for each I pray!

I'll welcome each day and also my gray,
And I'm glad there's no reason to weep.
I thank my Lord for helping me understand,
How for eternity my soul, He will keep.

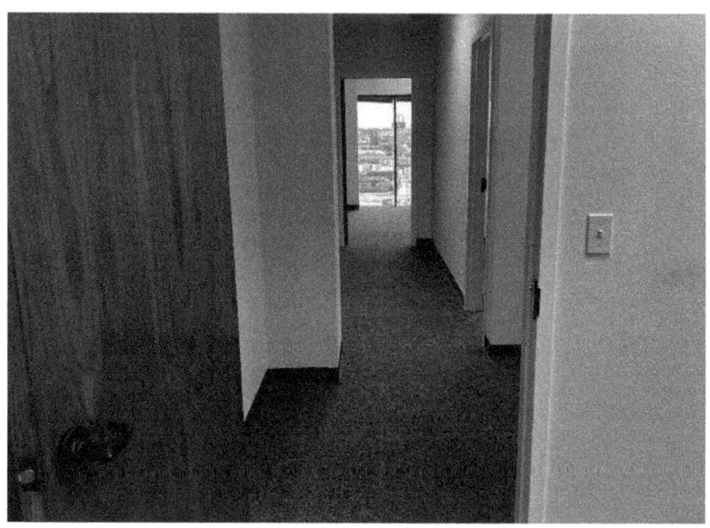

To a Very Special Person

Even though you're not a mother,
This Holiday is yours.
For you've shown your hope, and given your help,
Smiling through open doors.
So, except a token from a friend,
Who knows enough to say,
You've mothered people throughout the land,
 And still show it every day.

*This was written for a retired schoolteacher on
Mother's Day. After spending her life devoted to
teaching and her students, she got married for the
first time at the age of seventy-five.*

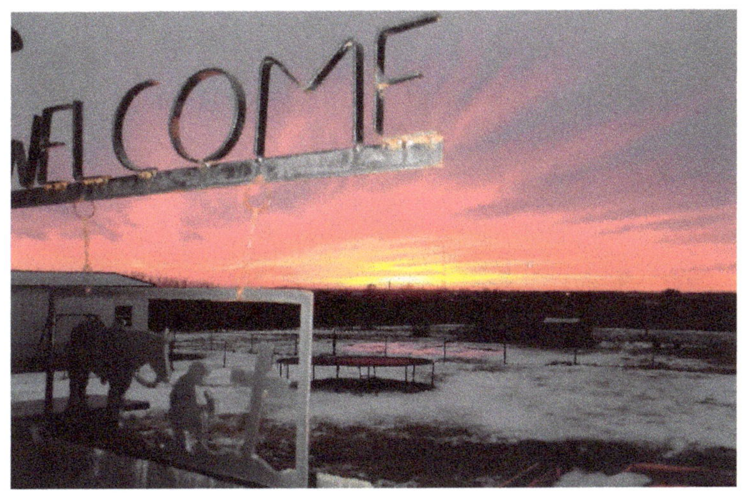

When My Time Comes

When the time comes, and my life is no more,
Remember me as I was.
Full of life, full of laughter,
And have a few tears just because.

My life on earth was brief.
I came to serve my Lord, Yahweh.
And now He will tell me if I did well,
As He welcomes me for each everlasting day.

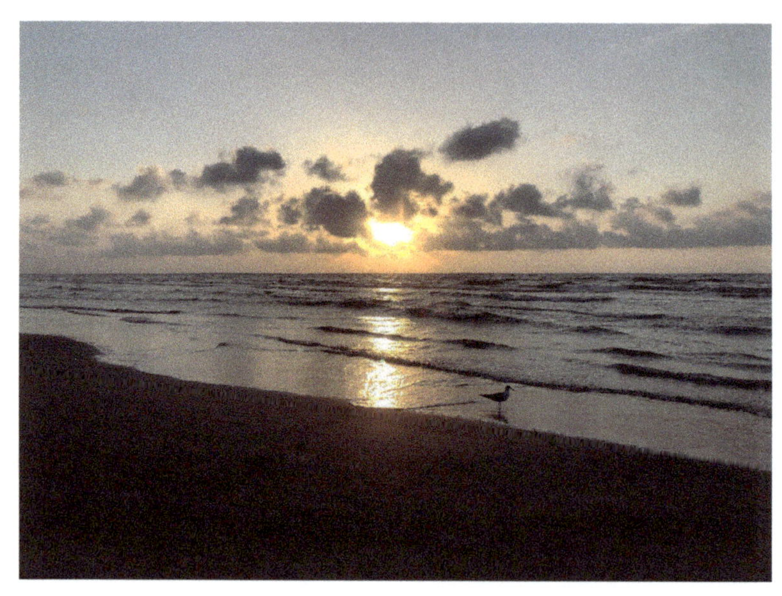

If I Should Die Before I Wake

Don't cry for me, I'm not there.

Uplift your life, that's where I care.

Try a little harder, do a little more.

I'm with you always just like before.

One day when you're thinking and feeling alone.

Remember for whom I lived. I'm at His throne!

For you to join me one day would be such a delight!

But you must pray to Jesus and ask Him into your life.

For now, spread my ashes to the sea.

And whenever you go there think of me.

Life is like the waves and tide.

Always coming in, going out, and moving side to side.

Just remember the One who put it all there.

And join me one day in heaven, that's what I care.

Life 2020

Blessed be the God and Father of our Lord Jesus Christ, the Father of mercies and God of all comfort, who comforts us in all our affliction, so that we may be able to comfort those who are in any affliction, with the comfort with which we ourselves are comforted by God (2 Corinthians 1:3-4 ESV).

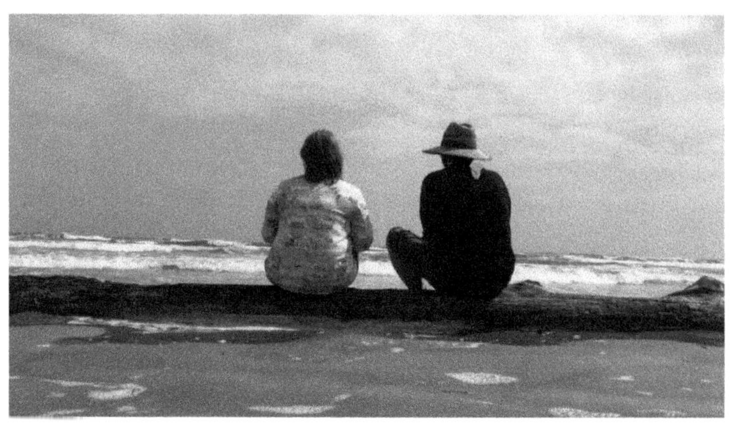

Only God is Real

This is a time when habits are broken.
When everything as we think it should be, is still.
And what we expect from our world is halted,
And only God is real.
This is a time to sit and ponder,
Instead of making plans.
To reflect on what we have and the world around us.
And to love our fellow man.
To everyone hurting and everyone lost,
I pray you'll find your peace.
But for now, for me, my family, and friends,
Please, let's all be on our knees.

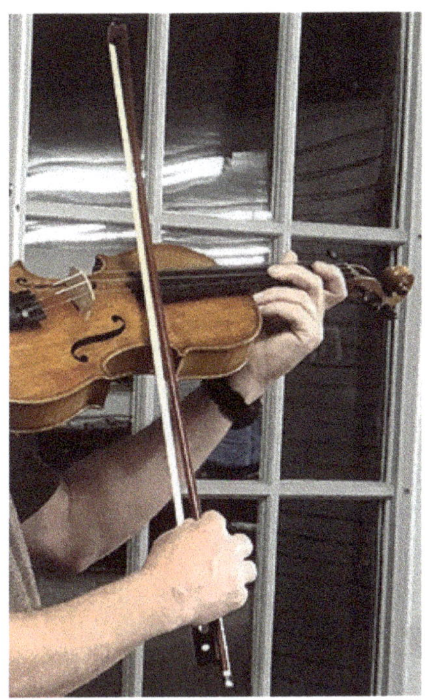

The Violin's Song

In New York, a violin plays,
At the corner of Althorp and Persia Way.
It starts at the end of each new day.
First responders of moms and dads,
Work long hours until everyone's needs are had.
Safety lurks but danger is near.
And the worst is what everyone fears.
The end will come, and we'll soon see you.
And hope this never starts anew.
As the violin plays, they meet again.
As we inspire each other to the very end.

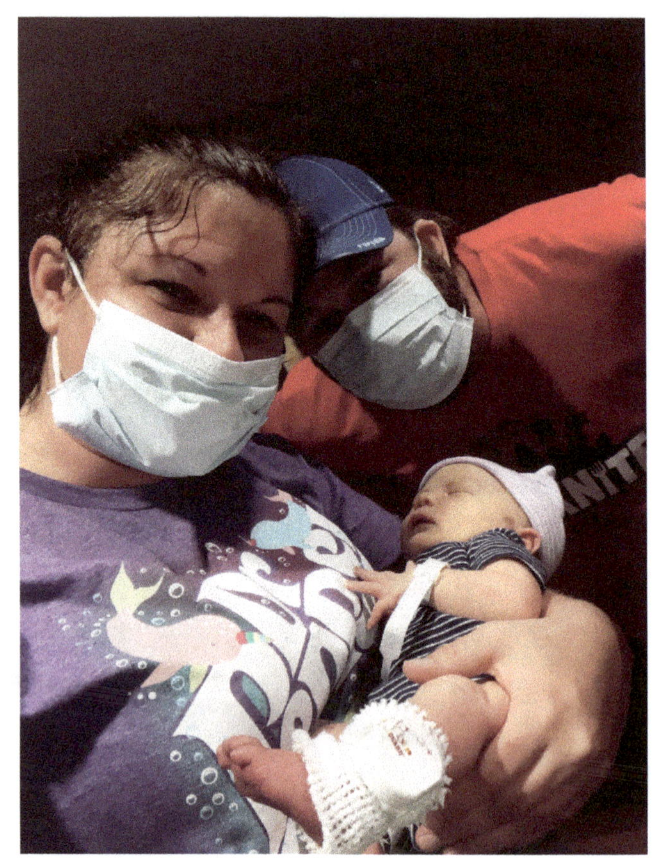

June 1, 2020

I'll be there in 2020 for you.
I tell you, my friend.
It will not be easy.
We will see things from a new view.
There will be time.
To reach toward the sublime.
And learn to refresh anew.
And I'll be there in 2020 for you.
We will learn new things.
And reach new heights.
As we contemplate darkness and night.
The days will seem long.
We won't all get along.
But I'll be there in 2020 for you.
Please remember to call.
Don't let yourself fall.
Together.
We can all this come through.
I'm here, this 2020, for you.

#newnormal2020, #love, #peace, #motivation,
#WeAreInThisTogether, #believe,
#forgivetoforgeforward, #unraveledtimetotell

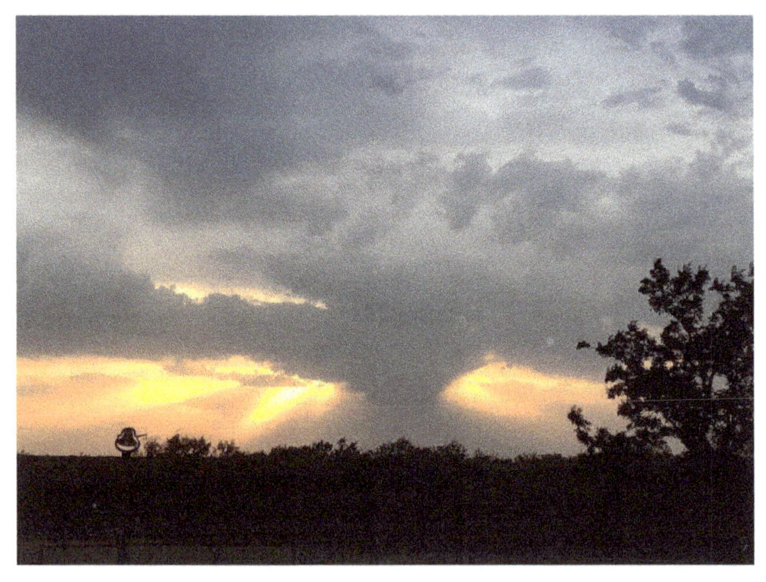

The Eye of the Storm

They sit waiting in the eye for the rest
Of the storm to attack.
They are getting over COVID, longing for
Normal life to be back.
I wait too, as my dad's in a home and
I want to see him.
But for all of us going through that storm,
We know for a while the chances are slim.
The nurses are good, and I know they care.
But he is stuck in his room,
Wishing I was there.
When will life resume to its old way?
Or will it ever, I hope and pray.
Please Lord, guide us and keep those safe,
Who are in harm's way.
We need your blessings to come and stay.
Pandemic, riots, and now,
record hurricane storms.
The plagues around 2020,
Have come in historic forms.
I know God has us in His hands through it all.
And I hope others will see Him,
Know this, and not fall.
Sin abounds when we're lost and scared.
Salvation occurs when Jesus is found,
And declared.
We need You like we have needed You before.
Please Lord, save us, your world restore.

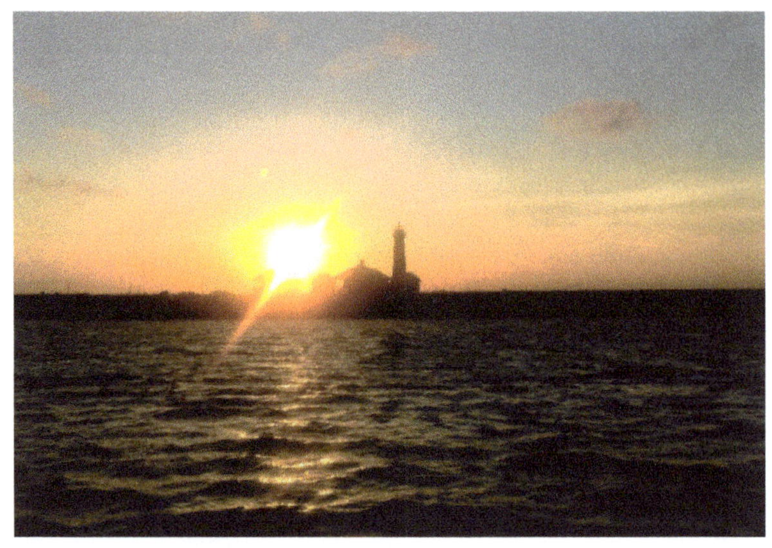

The Tears Are Dry

It has been a long hard year.
I wish I could cry.
But something inside me,
Makes the tears go dry.

Thank you, Lord,
For carrying me through.
Within your hands,
You lift me to something new.

At the end of the tunnel,
I see your light.
I humbly bow,
As it shines so bright!

Yes, it has been a hard year,
And it's left many in the dark.
They need you, Lord!
Put within them your Spirit's spark.

While here on earth,
I will not be afraid.
I will remember every day,
The tomb where my salvation laid.

I will praise you always,
For raising Him up.
To walk among us,
And fulfill His cup.

I thank you, God,
For Jesus, your son.
And for your forgiving, loving, mercy.
You gave for me and for everyone.

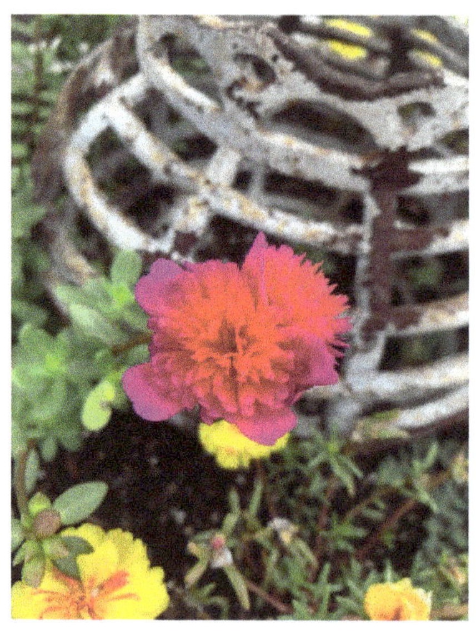

Pretty Flowers

He has made everything beautiful in its time. He has also set eternity in the hearts of men; yet they cannot fathom what God has done from beginning to end (Ecclesiastes 3:11 NIV).

We do not always see the beauty around us, especially right now, with this election, the pandemic, and all the social divisions going on. We might have to look outside of all the chaos in the quiet places. The quiet places like where the flowers grow. The beauty is not hidden. All we have to do is look for it. It is there. And when you find it be sure to give credit where credit is due.

Pretty flowers in my yard.
They come as sweet surprises.
They are in all different colors,
And many shapes and sizes.
I love the orange and yellow ones,
And I love the purple ones, too.
All of them standing so straight and tall,
Just for me and you.
Pretty flowers in my yard.
I would love to bring you in.
Where I can look in awe of you.
And feel myself blessed within.
God gave us the pretty flowers.
Because He doesn't want us sad.
But I'm sure He sees our hearts.
And sometimes gets unhappy and mad.
So, do not let the beauty hide,
Around you where you are.
Be sure to look because it's there.
And it is closer than the stars.

Thank you, God! Thank you for showing me beauty in the world and for eternity. All I need to do is see it and look with open eyes and a longing, seeking, heart. And thank You for making everything beautiful in its own time, in Your own time.

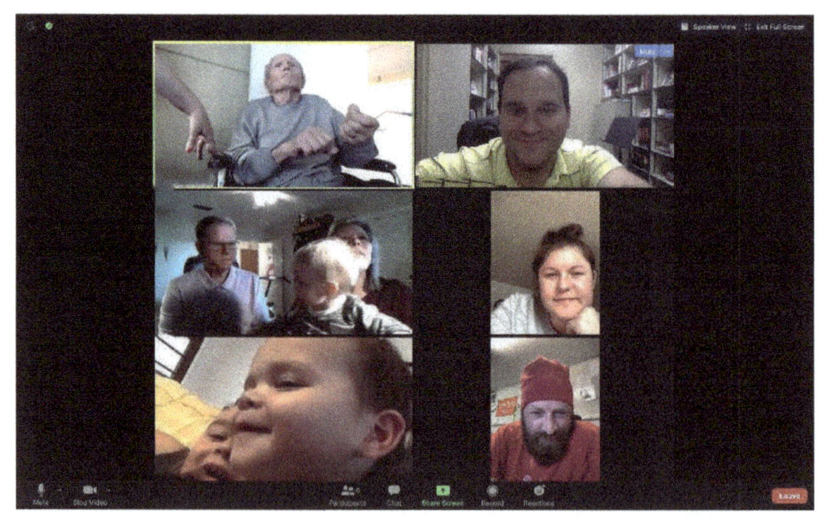

2020,
A Different Kind of Year

2020 has been different.
Different in so many ways.
No birthday candles, no cranberry sauce,
No family for so many days.

2020 has been unique,
An experience all its own.
When other time would you laugh and cry,
Over toilet paper, Lysol, and staying home.

2020 has been a year,
To share and love over Zoom.
And if you were left out from the group,
It wasn't for lack of room.

2020 has been a year.
A year we hope not to repeat.
But if you look back, you'll realize,
It's full of memories that can't be beat!

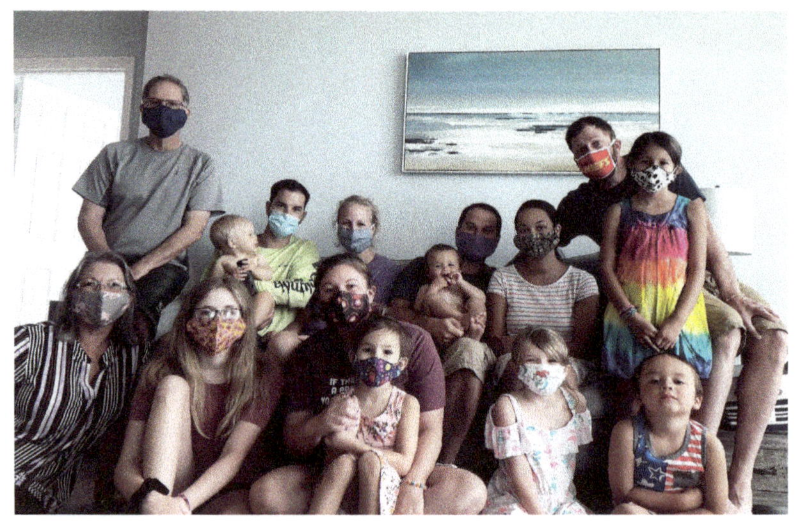

September 2020

Whether new or not,
The beginning will start.
Let us shout and praise,
With thanksgiving to our Lord.
This will all come to an end.
I pray we abound more than before,
Hopefully to fulfill God's goals.
And with prayer for our Lord to restore.

Lisa Lynn is a wife, mother, and grandma. She spent her childhood in a religious home until her mom was murdered, leaving her vulnerable and thrown into a new, evil world. She would then grow up seeking, searching, and studying the foundation her mother told her about, the saving grace of God through His Son, Jesus. She has written and led numerous Bible studies, classes, and public devotions for children, teens, adults, and elderly people and never misses an opportunity to speak about what God does in our lives. After years of keeping silent about her Momma and brother's unsolved murders, she told everything she could in her book, *Unraveled, Time to Tell.* She later wrote, *Unraveled, Time to Hear: An Investment toward Your Eternity,* which guides you to know more about God. She feels this book helped her to prepare her heart for the solving of the murders that would come fifty years after happening. Once she saw her own unforgiveness, she wrote, *Unraveled, Time to Forgive, A True Ending to Murder.* This book gives the end of the story as the truth about the murders was revealed.

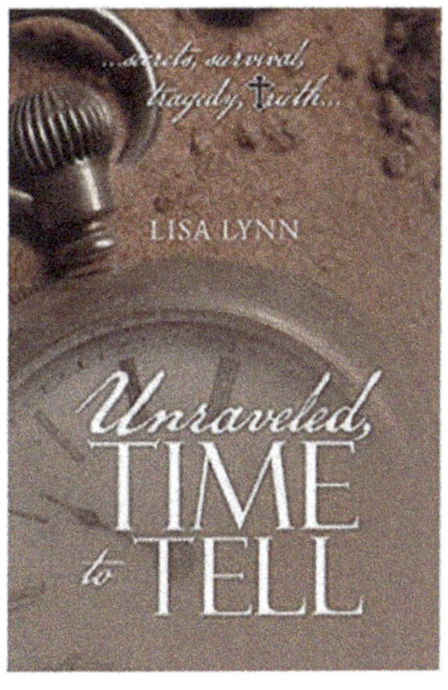
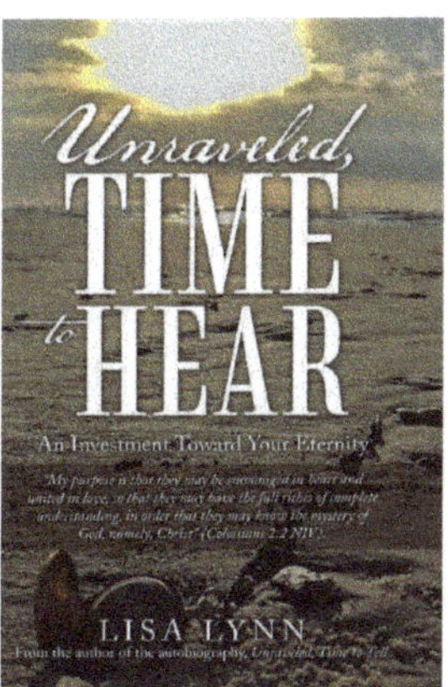
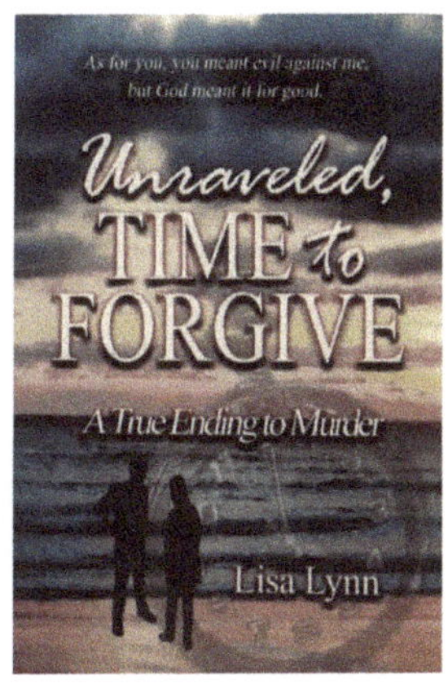